GOODNIGHT CHILDREN
. . . EVERYWHERE

GOODNIGHT CHILDREN
. . . EVERYWHERE

Ian Hartley

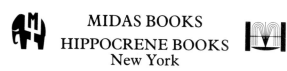 MIDAS BOOKS
HIPPOCRENE BOOKS
New York

First published in the UK in 1983 by
MIDAS BOOKS
44 Holden Park Road
Southborough, Kent TN4 0ER

ISBN 0 85936 201 9 (UK)

Published in the USA by
HIPPOCRENE BOOKS INC
171 Madison Avenue
New York, NY 10016

ISBN 0 88254 892 1

Printed in Great Britain by
Bookplan Limited

TO PRESENT CONSUMERS
STEPHEN AND PHILIP

CONTENTS

Acknowledgements

I would particularly like to thank David Davis, Daphne Oxenford and Edward Barnes for their time and recollections, and the BBC Archives Department, especially Jacqueline Kavanagh, for research facilities into their unique records. Thanks are also due to the staff of the Arts section of Manchester Central Library. I would like to acknowledge the advice and enthusiastic support of Geoffrey Clifton and Chris Davies, and the patience of my wife Sheilagh. Finally, my thanks go to all the 'uncles' and 'aunts', not all of whom have been mentioned in this book, but without whom so many of our childhoods would have been the poorer.

Foreword

In these days of great and rapid changes in our lives I feel it is important, if not essential, to keep hold of fundamental simplicities. One of the these is that children love to be told stories. If we look back through history and literature, it is clear that there have always been storytellers. In Victorian times of course children's stories always had to have a moral (how daunting!), but I have read that the favourite request to mothers or grandparents was 'Tell me about when you were little'. Because young people today are more sophisticated and exposed to more technology than in our parents' days, the tales of our own extreme youth can seem to our children like something from the Middle Ages – 'Was there really life before television?'

In this book Ian Hartley celebrates (and I use the word advisedly) the enormous contribution made by the BBC and, latterly, ITV to children's entertainment, enjoyment and (dare I use the word?) culture.

The BBC first broadcast the Children's Hour in December 1922, and since that time the Corporation has continued to cater for what will be its adult audience of tomorrow. To someone of my generation, what memories are conjured up by reading about birthday greetings, the Toytown stories (Larry the Lamb, Mr Mayor, Dennis the Dachshund), Winnie the Pooh (Norman Shelley singing 'How Sweet To Be a Cloud'), and of course the immortal words of the title of this book – 'Goodnight children . . . everywhere' – as inspired and well-loved a phrase as 'Are you sitting comfortably?'

I was privileged to be one of the storytellers on *Listen With Mother* for twenty-one of the thirty-two years of its life, and it was evident to us all on the programme that its strength was the knowledge of what was wanted by its audience. Not only was there the constant repetition of well-loved songs and nursery rhymes (and since the demise of Nursery Sing-Song along with Children's Hour, it was the only place where the traditional rhymes could be heard), but the stories were varied and the most popular ones were requested over and over again. Among these were 'Jacko the

7

Monkey', 'Mitten the Kitten', 'Dan the Pig', 'Tommy the Tugboat' and 'My Naughty Little Sister'.

To those who might deplore change and feel that the stories of, for example, Dr Who lack the simplicity and naive charm of the early broadcast programmes, I would say only that children still ask for stories, either to read themselves or, better still, to be read to them. So long as this demand is there, writers will continue to write, programme makers will continue to produce material for transmission by radio or television and, perhaps most important of all, parents will tell their own stories to their children – stories which (who knows?) might be treasured from their own childhood delights.

Daphne Oxenford

Introduction

Let me say at the outset that I have no qualifications to embark on such a book as this other than that of a delighted consumer. The reason for this nostalgic trip into my own and, I hope, your childhood memories is threefold. First, very little has been written about the pioneers or the development of children's radio and television. Second, I have always been pleased to be reminded of old memories in many spheres of entertainment, and the chance to jog the memory of others was an exciting prospect. And third – perhaps the real reason – I have such fond memories of my childhood and of the stories, adventures, music and humour brought into my home through broadcasting that it was more than a labour of love to relive those times in my research.

I am not one of the 'better when I was a lad' brigade, as I can see the vast scope of entertainment and education with which television delights my children today. Perhaps the imagination is not stimulated as much as when listening to those adventures of Biggles or walks with Romany, perhaps some of the cosiness is lost; but the variety, the effort and the enjoyment seem, if my children are anything to go by, greater than ever. They will still sit, however, and listen to records of 'Three Billygoats Gruff', 'I Taut I Taw a Puddy Tat', 'Me and my Teddy Bear' and many others I enjoyed as a child. Perhaps some things never date. Certainly, even alongside the sophistication of today's entertainment, the slapstick comedy of the silent film and the circus clown can still amuse.

I have not dwelt on the sociological aspects of viewing and listening as I feel many better qualified than I have done so; the list of further reading will help anyone who wishes to pursue this aspect of the genre. I hope I have been able to give some indication, however, of the use and misuse of this particularly dominant aspect of one's most formative years.

Whatever the period of your childhood, I hope you will be able to find in this book programmes, personalities and times you remember with affection, and be as interested as I have been to trace the evolution of children's broadcasting. So if you're sitting comfortably, I'll begin.

1
Waves in the Ether

The Marconi Wireless Telegraph & Signal Company was founded in 1897, and created something of a stir among those companies then operating 'wire telegraphy', with (as we now realise) some justification. The company, overcoming both scepticism and technical difficulties, was eventually able to pay dividends to its shareholders in 1911. By that time Marconi had a virtual monopoly of the technique in Italy, Canada and England. By 1914 several transmissions of speech and music had been received some hundred miles away from their source, Marconi House in London. In the Marconi Chelmsford factory 'wireless telephone sets' which had a reception radius of at least thirty miles were already being manufactured.

The activity in invention and manufacture was matched by feverish political argument over all aspects of this new phenomenon; over its consequences and, more often than not, over the Marconi Company itself. On the outbreak of war in 1914, the Admiralty took over wireless production at the Marconi works and, as happened in other spheres, caused an acceleration in development. Experiments and arguments continued after the war, but in late 1921 the Marconi Company was allowed to 'broadcast' calibration signals to amateurs for half an hour a week.

The first regular broadcast was made on 14 February 1922 from a hut at Marconi's Writtle station (2MT) near Chelmsford. Captain Peter Eckersley led the enthusiastic team at Writtle, playing records, acting, singing and chatting to his select audience and uttering the station call sign in his own unique style: 'This is Two Emma Toc Writtle Testing'. He was later to become the BBC's first chief engineer.

In the Metropolitan Vickers Electrical Company's factory in Trafford Park, Manchester, station 2ZY soon began operations also. This Anglo-American-owned company was Marconi's first rival. The second was the Western Electric Company's 5IT in Birmingham.

In the United States, radio stations were springing up without the restraining influence of a Government and Post Office determined not to be hurried. The British Government did not wish to have the responsibility of

A . R. Burrows (Uncle Arthur) at the 'meatsafe' microphone in the London 2LO studio. Originally a journalist, he wrote an article entitled 'Wireless Possibilities' in the 1918 Yearbook of Wireless Telegraphy and Wireless Telephony. *After working at the Marconi Chelmsford works, including arranging the broadcast by Dame Nellie Melba, he became Director of Programmes for the British Broadcasting Company in 1922.*

providing its own broadcasting service, but was reluctant to allow the proliferation of local stations. A franchise system was the initial method discussed – to allow stations to operate with their revenue coming from licences. In practice, the Post Office left it to the main companies involved to reach agreement among themselves as to who had which station and where. When agreement between them was not forthcoming, the Post Office was forced to step in, and created the British Broadcasting Company (BBC) as a monopoly.

The BBC began daily broadcasts in November 1922: from 2LO at Marconi House, in the Strand, London on the 14th, and from Manchester (2ZY) and Birmingham (5IT) on the 15th. This was the very day of the second post-war General Election. The results were broadcast by the BBC; by a cruel twist of fate Postmaster-General F. G. Kellaway, who had been thought most likely to become the BBC's first general manager, lost his seat.

It was John Charles Walsham Reith, a 34-year-old Scottish engineer, who instead became general manager (and later managing director). The company had been constituted with a capital of £100,000, of which £60,000 was provided, in equal proportions, by six large electrical and wireless manufacturers.

In the homes of southern England enthusiasts began to manipulate their 'cat's whiskers' searching for that small voice. A. J. Alan described his first wireless set as 'a whole lot of coils and condensers screwed down on a board. The detector was electrolytic, made out of a potted-meat jar, a piece of carbon rod and a glass stylo-filler . . . but it worked, and the first signal that came through gave me no end of a thrill.' Valve sets were available for those who thought that radio was here to stay, but a four-valve set could cost as much as fifty pounds in the 1920s. Valve sets had better reception than the crystal sets, but had the disadvantage that their batteries had to be regularly recharged, which involved trips to the local dealer.

In 1923, the BBC moved into the Institution of Electrical Engineers building in Savoy Hill, because of the cramped studio conditions at Marconi House. An agreement was made the following year with Selfridges store by which the BBC was to pay Selfridges 'an annual sum of ten shillings (if demanded) by way of rent' to allow a transmitter on their roof.

The move by the BBC to its own custom-built headquarters, Broadcasting House, was not to come until 1932. That building has remained a famous London landmark to the present day.

The first stations in London, Manchester and Birmingham were soon joined by Cardiff, Glasgow, Aberdeen, Bournemouth, Sheffield, Plymouth, Edinburgh, Liverpool, Leeds, Bradford, Hull, Nottingham, and others. The policy of regional stations was adopted for both technical and organisational reasons, and in fact children's broadcasts were provided on a purely regional basis for many years.

After recommendations of the Crawford Committee were accepted in 1926, the British Broadcasting Company was replaced from New Year's

LISTENIN'!

First result after two hours tickling the cat's whisker.

"All stations of the B.B.C. are now closing down, good night everybody—good night!"

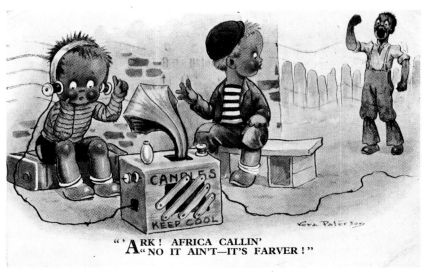

"'ARK! AFRICA CALLIN'
"NO IT AIN'T—IT'S FARVER!"

Some early attempts at tuning in on the wireless.

Day 1927 by the British Broadcasting Corporation, constituted under Royal Charter. Reith became Director-General, and under his control the Corporation developed into a vast organisation with the 'public service' attitude at the heart of all its activities. The original company had attempted to acquire revenue from both a ten-shilling receiving licence and taxes from radio equipment, but the latter were dropped and, for better or worse, the only revenue for the developing BBC was from the licence and from its own publications.

In 1926, the old company had shown its determination not to become an arm of government when at the time of the General Strike several voices, including that of Winston Churchill, urged for more control of the media. Its independence was maintained with a certain degree of voluntary censorship, with Reith steering a careful but determined course through political upheaval.

A glance at the programmes in those early years reveals a rather sombre, instructive theme. Reith disliked variety shows and much popular music and this, with the reluctance of many theatrical impresarios to allow their contracted stars to appear on radio, provided little light relief to the listening public. However, it was Reith's policy that the 'Children's Corner' should not be just an extension of the classroom, but an interesting as well as informative branch of the service. Schools broadcasting, though it had many critics when it began, established itself as a useful addition to the teacher's educational aids, while from very early in BBC history the Children's Hour provided amusement, excitement, wonder and often a social focus with the Radio Circles of ardent young listeners.

Manufacturers of radios and components, such as E. K. Cole (Ekco), Atlas, Amplion, Lissen and Celestion promised 'rewarding performance', 'perfect reproduction' or made other similar claims, but by today's standards the quality was crude. For reasonable reception a long aerial was required, and the urban landscape was transformed by numerous lengths of cable draped across back gardens. A listener's licence allowed up to one hundred feet of wire to be used!

2
Early Disorganisation

It was on 5 December 1922 that A. E. Thompson, an engineer on the Birmingham station, made broadcasting history by presenting a few minutes' entertainment 'just for children'. He told a story of Spick and Span, two dwarfs, and played a gramophone record called 'Dance of the Goblins'. He subsequently became Uncle Thompson. Other stations followed Birmingham's lead and on Saturday 23 December the very first Children's Hour was broadcast from the London station. There was very little planning in the first programmes and the organisation was a somewhat haphazard affair; but Reith's aim 'to provide an hour of clean, wholesome humour, some light music and a judicious sprinkling of information, attractively conveyed' was always the fundamental objective.

One of the lesser-known poems of Henry Wadsworth Longfellow was the original source of the title given to the children's section of broadcasting. It begins:

> *Between the dark and the daylight,*
> *When the night is beginning to lower,*
> *Comes a pause in the day's occupations,*
> *That is known as the Children's Hour.*

Certainly, at the start those concerned with these programmes did regard it as a pause between their normal tasks. The contributors were any members of the stations' staff who felt they could supply something, whether it be a song, a story, or just add to the 'jolly spirit'.

The duration of the Hour soon settled down to a regular forty-five minutes, and no one person was given the responsibility of supervising it. A. R. Burrows, who as Marconi's publicity manager had arranged that company's Marconi House broadcasts, soon took charge of all the BBC's London programmes. It was he who wrote the first ever play for broadcasting, called *The Truth about Father Christmas*, which was broadcast on Christmas Eve 1922. Mrs Harman Earl, a voluntary worker, provided material for the early Hours, but many consisted of unscripted

Children's Hour at 2LO: Uncle Rex, Aunt Sophie, Uncle Caractacus. In cramped studio conditions, made acoustically dead and oppressive by layers of material on the walls, the early contributors made merry with pioneering enthusiasm.

backchat, which was later to annoy many critics. Burrows, recollecting his later role as Uncle Arthur, described the atmosphere of those early shows as 'not a romp of incoherent noise, but a communal outpouring of happiness'. In his book *Broadcasting from Within*, C. A. Lewis (Uncle Caractacus) also writes of the studio atmosphere in glowing terms, describing how, after the rigours of the day 'we join together at 5.30 to forget the quarrels, the difficulties, the vested interests, because here at least we are free of them'. It was a place where 'one could be foolish without being a fool'.

The Corner became established as a permanent and popular part of the daily programmes and, with a rapidly growing audience, an official at each station was given the task of its organisation. On 5 April 1923 Mrs Ella Fitzgerald was appointed as central organiser of Children's Hour for London and the provinces. A month later she also took responsibility for Woman's Hour. In December she was joined by Miss E. Elliott (Auntie Geraldine), who was appointed as her assistant, and Miss R. May, who looked after the clerical work of what was now becoming a slightly more disciplined activity.

It was stated at a station directors' meeting in December that contributors should be given set times to broadcast and that more preparation was to go into the transmissions. It was felt that by giving aunts and uncles more time to prepare material, with set days, their contributions would be of greater substance than the spontaneous

17

offerings that were currently being attempted. Mrs Fitzgerald was also given the task of visiting the provincial stations from time to time. In Birmingham she found Percy Edgar (Uncle Edgar) running the station and personally presiding over the Children's Hour. In Manchester, Kenneth Wright was the first station manager, engineer, announcer, director and, as Uncle Humpty Dumpty, was looking after the children's broadcasts too. Dan Godfrey Junior later succeeded him.

In the London studio Uncle Caractacus ran the Hour, with Mrs Fitzgerald supplying material but rarely taking part. With Stanton Jefferies (Uncle Jeff) and Rex Palmer (Uncle Rex) they formed 'our happy triumvirate', as Lewis called them. Uncle Rex, London station director, took over the Children's Hour responsibility in April 1924. Earlier in that year a Children's Hour committee had been formed to advise on programme content and speakers, but after only a few meetings, producing little in the way of constructive suggestions, it disbanded.

There was criticism in the Press about the backchat and 'unprofessionalism' in the Hour, and C. F. G. Masterman wrote in *Radio Times* that the programmes were amateurish; that there were no stars; that there was too much childish chatter, which he said the children disliked, and that many of the items were too 'heavy' for youngsters. The 'kiddiwinkie' attitude still existed at many stations, with a Kiddies' Corner at Birmingham and Kiddies' Grotto at Manchester.

In February 1925 the Programme Board suggested a reorganisation of the Hour especially to reduce backchat. Again steps were taken to put one person in overall charge, but this time it was to be his sole duty. C. E. Hodges (Uncle Peter) was appointed in April to take entire charge. (Mrs Fitzgerald was by now totally involved in women's programmes.) In September J. C. Stobart became education director overseeing the Children's Hour Department. As had been suggested some time earlier, a daily rota of staff was established and a more systematic approach finally arrived, at least in London.

It fell to Mr Stobart to house the only pet that BBC radio ever kept. A parrot was obtained in the hope that it would become a 'regular' on the programmes. Several attempts were made, in front of the microphone, to make the wretched bird talk or even make a noise – all to no avail. It was a dismal failure as an artist and, after pining for some weeks, passed away.

The regions were still organising their own Hours, and whole 'families' of aunts and uncles were becoming popular with their listeners. There were Uncle Clarence and Aunt Jean in Plymouth, Auntie Mollie in Edinburgh, and in London Phyllis Thomas (Auntie Phyllis) and Cecile Dixon (Auntie Sophie). The last of these had trained at the Royal College of Music and, after meeting Stanton Jefferies, began broadcasting almost as a joke. She became accompanist in London and is often remembered by her signature tune, 'Country Gardens'.

In 1925 Eric Fogg became station accompanist in Manchester, and as

18

Uncle Eric he became a firm favourite. Glasgow had Uncle Mungo and Auntie Cyclone, whose inspired name was changed to Auntie Kathleen (her real name) after memoranda from London to Mr Marshall, the station director. Auntie Kathleen was Miss Garscadden, who became the driving force in Glasgow for many years. She always tried to end the early programmes with a lullaby:

> *Hush-a-bye, hush-a-bye, close your sleepy eyes,*
> *Fairies now are calling you – calling from the skies,*
> *Slumberland, slumberland 'neath a dreaming moon.*
> *Baby's gone to lead the way,*
> *Daddy's coming soon.*

Auntie Doris (Doris Gambell) began her long association with children's programmes in Liverpool, while Nottingham had a wicked Uncle Laurie who kept 'interfering' with Auntie Ruby. In Stoke-on-Trent Uncle Leslie, Jack Frost (Captain Frost) and Uncle Pollard (Pollard Crowther) gathered a following as early as 1923 with their technical and travel talks. Auntie Vi (Violet Fraser – the first Auntie Vi in the North) and Uncle Victor (Victor Smythe) were regulars in Manchester. Things did not always go quite smoothly. The *Manchester Evening News* recently quoted Reginald Jordan, who was one of the early 2ZY pioneers, who remembers: 'I was horror-struck one Saturday when in the middle of Kiddies' Corner I heard a tipsy voice say, "Hello – hic – kiddies. Uncle Bod calling, Uncle Bod calling".' The uncle was merry on Boddington's ale! Swearing was, of course, unthinkable, but Jordan also remembered one engineer, who insisted on ending his occasional talks with a kiss to the youngsters. Forgetting to throw the necessary switch when he finished one of his talks, over the air was heard, 'That's finished with the little buggers till Monday, thank God!'

A London Children's Hour Programme Board was instituted, having its first meeting on 12 November 1926. The meeting was chaired by Roger Eckersley (younger brother of Captain Eckersley). Among its proposals were that the terms 'auntie' and 'uncle' should be dropped at once. The terms had disappeared from the pages of *Radio Times* some time earlier. It was thought that the titles were undignified for staff of the BBC. There were protests from both children and parents and, although no longer encouraged, the soubriquets were allowed to linger on. In the 1934 *BBC Year Book* William Moffat wrote that in the early days of radio 'there was nothing undignified or incongruous then in station leaders assuming the role of "uncle" every afternoon for the amusement of children, and the intimacy established in this and other ways between officials and listeners was of incalculable value to the new company and the objects for which it stood'.

It is certain that the contributors enjoyed their roles. One, Uncle Pat from the Birmingham station, wrote in the very first *Hullo Boys Annual* in 1924 about the songs, some seventy each week, that they performed. He

HULLO BOYS!

A BUDGET OF GOOD THINGS BY
THE UNCLES ON THE WIRELESS

"**HERE WE ARE AGAIN!**"

Published by the Courtesy of the B.B.C. by

CECIL PALMER
49 CHANDOS STREET, W.C.2

'The uncles on the wireless' – and the aunts – soon reached young readers too, with the Hullo Boys *and* Hullo Girls *annuals, first published in 1924.*

described a rehearsal: 'Just imagine in the Train Song our noble station director (Uncle Edgar) making "choo-choo" noises on the drums, with the most staid of musical directors (Uncle Joe) blowing the supposed train whistle, while Uncle Bonzo (late commander of a destroyer squadron) makes noises of shutting carriage doors.

20

Mr. R. F. PALMER.
(" Uncle Rex.")

"HULLO! Children, everywhere!" You know the old, familiar signal, of course. But this time you can read it in nice black print, instead of hearing it through the microphone. That will be a change — sounds different, eh? I mean, looks different. Now, what do I really mean? I cannot think how to put it, but you know what I mean, so we will leave it at that. And that's that!

Anyhow, I am jolly glad to have an opportunity of telling you all sorts of secrets, and other things, about the treats which are being prepared for you during the coming winter. You will be pleased, I think; and if you are pleased, all your broadcasting Uncles and Aunts—and you are going to have several more soon—will be pleased, too, for I can assure you that everybody at the B.B.C. stations looks forward eagerly to the Children's Hour, as it is the happiest hour of the busy days which are spent in making arrangements for your entertainment.

A Splendid Secret.

And now for a great secret! Hush! Not a word!

Probably, before long, your Uncles will be able to talk to you sometimes while you are at school; for I must tell you that in future you will have more time given to you. The Children's Hour will always remain as it is at present; for it is so popular that no change can be made. But you may have another hour, or more, earlier in the day!

How would you like to have real lessons given you at school by your Uncles? That may be done—but you must be patient, and just wait and see what will happen. We shall, I hope, make you want to know more and more about all the subjects.

You see, children, I have taken you into our confidence; and I want you to take us into your confidence. If there is anything you would like to hear about, or any kind of entertainment you would like to have, just write and tell us all about it. Your Uncles will, with great pleasure to themselves, try to give you what you want to have.

Extracts from 'Children's Corner' in the very first Radio Times *(28 September 1923), including an early indication of what was to become schools broadcasting.*

21

'In the Farmyard Song things sometimes get very mixed. Instead of hearing the donkey doing his "hee-haw" someone makes the neigh of a horse (I won't say who) and in the concluding line, in place of a "cock-a-doodle-doo", it has been said that the sound of a large black Thomas cat comes over. However, it's all in the fun of the day.'

Alan Howland (Uncle Columbus) became Head of Children's Hour in January 1929 when Hodges left. After three years he too left the BBC, but returned as an announcer in the war. Some of the aunts and uncles had more than a transient influence, some working for the department for several decades. May E. Jenkin (Elizabeth), Derek McCulloch (Uncle Mac) and David Davis (David) on the London staff devoted much of their lives to entertaining generations of youngsters, and the provinces could also boast staunch regulars, referred to later.

It had been proposed that the BBC should produce a children's magazine. This was to be a miniature *Radio Times* containing details of children's programmes along with other articles, but after various attempts to assess the viability of such a project it was decided to settle for a children's page in *Radio Times* itself. This had been attempted as early as 1923 with various uncles contributing. Uncle Caractacus had edited the page at first and then found himself writing the bulk of it.

The new page contained news of children's programmes and regular articles from several Children's Hour presenters. H. Mortimer Batten wrote on all things natural, Craven Hill wrote about animals, Alwin Gissing told of his adventures, and Stephen King-Hall wrote about the ways of the world. R. T. Gould (the Star Gazer) wrote authoritatively on almost everything under the sun. Gould, six feet four inches tall and weighing seventeen stone, was larger than life and had a rich store of personal knowledge to impart. His articles as well as his broadcasts were about his many interests and hobbies, which included chronometers, collecting typewriters and mechanical toys, making helicopters and investigating enigmas, oddities, sea serpents and other monsters – in fact just what children's dreams are made of. Derek McCulloch supplied an article for several years under the title 'Hullo Children' which sometimes contained news of forthcoming programmes, but more often than not was about 'what I did this week'; this continued until 1935.

3
A Jolly Good Time

Broadcasting to children had, of course, no precedents and presented certain peculiar difficulties. There was the difficulty of deciding at just what level to pitch the programmes, because what may be interesting to a five-year-old may bore an older child and vice versa. The interests of boys and girls would also differ in many ways. The organisers realised that they were trying to entertain a section of the public with probably the widest distribution of intelligence, experience, interests and tastes. Inevitably there was compromise, but in the main the attempt to entertain an age range from five to early teens succeeded.

The second difficulty was to decide what was a good programme. Ideally it should not have a 'school out of school' atmosphere, but still be worthwhile in the child's most impressionable years. In the *BBC Handbook* of 1928 the standing orders for such programmes are quoted, and put quite succinctly what must surely be the premise on which all future children's broadcasting has been based. They state: 'If the organisers of Children's Hour keep in mind the creation of the atmosphere of a good home and the presentation of real beauty in song, story, music and poetry on a plane attractive to the young, they will inevitably, without self-conscious effort, raise the standard of culture in their young listeners and as a result will be educative in the best sense.'

The earliest programme listings were published in Selfridges advertisements in *The Pall Mall Gazette*, and it was some months (28 September 1923) before *Radio Times* first appeared. In its programme schedules for children we find the London station presenting stories by Herbert Strange and Helen Bannerman, while Uncle Donald told stories on the Cardiff station. Newcastle also transmitted a thirty-minute talk under the heading *Scholars' Half Hour*, and this idea was repeated later by some other stations. Most also carried a Boys' Brigade news item. By 1923 occasional 'simultaneous broadcasts' were relayed from other regions, but programme sharing was still in its infancy.

Programmes were obviously geared to the middle-class child, with more

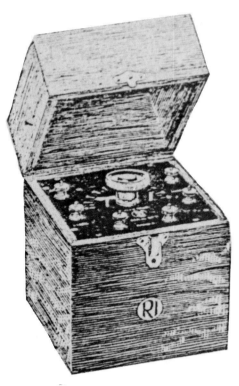

Crystal set 'for the kiddies', at £2-2-0 complete. At the cinema children were still watching silent films, but with a long enough aerial and an effective earth (e.g. a drainpipe) they could hear the magic of sound transmitted to their own homes.

serious than lighthearted music. The presenters were, however, able to send themselves up sometimes, with Stanton Jefferies becoming 'Aunt Priscilla' and giving talks on 'voice culture' or etiquette.

One of the most prominent features on the Hours in the 1920s was the fairy story. There was a Fairy League in Newcastle, and Edinburgh began its time for young children with the 'bells of Fairyland'. In a memorandum to C. E. Hodges in February 1927, Roger Eckersley asked disdainfully: 'How much of the fairytale stuff are you actually doing now?' In the same memo he suggested that they were not doing enough for the older children. At about this time a note was prepared to be sent to the station directors, stressing that they should recognise the importance of the Hour and the difficulties of variations in age, social status, taste and environment that had to be borne in mind when preparing programmes. The directors were advised to avoid 'babyish' items and abolish backchat and, of course, the terms 'aunt' and 'uncle' were not to be used. They were also informed that 'the word "child" should be construed as the ordinary boy or girl of ten to twelve, living in a good middle-class home and attending a good school'.

Programmes gradually became better planned, and even rehearsed! Personalities from outside the BBC were invited to give talks on sport, animals and current affairs. Dance music was heard. (The suggestion of having dancing lessons was not taken up when it was realised that most people were still listening on headphones.) The criterion used for assessing whether any item should not be included was solely 'Can it harm children?', and the station directors could use their own discretion.

For many years, a large chunk of the transmissions was taken up with birthday greetings. These had begun in London in 1923 and became extremely popular. At first any child's name could be called, often with

A vicar's views in 'Listeners' Letters' in the Radio Times *of 6 November 1925.*

Do You Like the Children's Hour?

I HAVE just read Mrs. Masterman's article on the Children's Hour in *The Radio Times*, and I am rash enough to differ entirely from the views expressed therein.

First, what do we mean by "children"? Surely not the precocious youths and maidens in their 'teens who look down upon those a few years younger as "kids." Let these listen with the "grown ups." Please, B.B.C., cater for children.

Next, as to the programmes. For Heaven's sake don't turn them into performances!

At present, the most delightful and valuable feature of "the hour" is its air of naturalness and homeliness. The "Uncle" and "Aunt" idea is excellent. Keep up the illusion whatever you do. Don't turn Uncle and Aunt into *compère* and *commère* of revue. And the "idiotic" backchat (so *natural,* you know!) is delightful from its spontaneity. Real children do not appreciate set and rehearsed fun, however clever, half as much as the little obvious quips that crop up at the moment, and an Auntie's natural chuckle at an unexpected remark is worth a lot of rehearsed "fun."

I admit that I am no longer a child, but having been in Orders over thirty years, I may claim to have been brought into contact with many hundreds of children of all ages and classes, and I feel sure I am voicing the wishes of the little ones in the above remarks.

The general broadcast covers the older children's needs. Do keep the children's hour for the real little ones.—PHILIP MULHOLLAND, Stapleford Vicarage, Salisbury.

instructions about where they might find hidden presents. As audiences increased, this section of the programmes became overlong and it was decided to stop it in 1924 and use it solely for sick children. However, to have one's birthday broadcast was one of the advantages of membership of a Radio Circle and there was naturally an outcry.

Such was the response that the birthday greetings were resumed, but confined to a strict time limit, with sick children taking precedence, and so still over the air waves came the calls of 'Hello . . . twins!' and 'Hello . . . trrriplets!' Eventually sheer numbers made the feature totally impracticable to organise, and the last congratulations were broadcast on 31 December 1933; the last two children to have that honour were Paul and Prudence Champion of Forest Gate. That last birthday list, preserved in the BBC archives, still bears the handwritten notes in the margin against a child's name: 'sick', 'in hospital', 'poorly'.

Letters from children and their parents were useful to the programme planners in those early days. During 1926, for example, some 54,334 letters were received at the London and Daventry Children's Hours. Of those, only twenty-two contained adverse comments, while 9000 were complimentary. Throughout the years the organisers of children's programmes have set great store by the comments and suggestions of listeners and viewers. Those first planners were much encouraged by the favourable response, and a very close relationship grew up between uncles, aunts and their young audience. There was the now famous letter from a child who wrote that she liked the wireless better than the theatre because the scenery was better! Even as early as 1922 Percy Edgar in Birmingham was receiving six letters a day. One year later the mail had risen to over a hundred letters a day.

It was in one of those letters (in April 1923) that a little girl suggested a club should be formed for young listeners, and this came about under the name of the Birmingham Radio Circle. The idea quickly spread to the other regions and became nearly an institution in itself. By 1928 the membership in Birmingham alone was over 10,000.

The original membership fee was one shilling, and this gave life membership as well as a badge. After four years, however, an annual subscription was substituted. The chief function of the Circles, apart from encouraging ties between the children and the BBC, was to motivate youngsters to devote time to good causes in their areas and 'to turn to altruistic usefulness the vast amount of energy presented by some thousands of children'. There was even a Doggie Circle in Glasgow; the dogs wore a badge on their collars.

The Radio Circle badges became standardised to the design originally used by Cardiff and Swansea. This showed the rays of the sun with a rabbit and cockerel in the foreground. The sun-ray motif lead to some regions calling their followers Radio Sunbeams, and each member had to make the following promises:

The badge for members of the Radio Circle in the BBC's North Region. Members were sometimes invited to functions such as picnic trips. One such trip, to Edale, was organised by the North Region on 24 September 1927, and members were reminded on the invitation not to forget their raincoats. In the Midlands, regular Saturday afternoon concerts were organised. In all areas attempts were made to form close ties between broadcasters and their young audiences.

1. To do all I can to keep cheerful and happy.
2. To do my best to bring delight into the lives of other children.
3. To be kind to animals.
4. To try to make my home, school and surroundings beautiful: and certainly not to throw any rubbish such as crockery, tins, papers, etc., into the streets about my home, or in the countryside.
5. To look for beauty in books, pictures and in all things of our daily life; and to be a loyal member of the ring of Radio Sunbeams.

Numerous charitable projects were undertaken by Circle members. Many of the early Circles provided hospitals with wireless sets for children's wards. When the Radio Circles were disbanded charitable work still continued, and annual appeals raised thousands of pounds. In 1943, for example, the Children's Hour director handed over a mobile X-ray unit to the British Red Cross, paid for by £3500 of the £15,000 received from Uncle Mac's appeal. The rest went to several hospitals to provide facilities for children. During the six years up to the end of the war the annual children's appeals raised £60,000.

As early as 1925 Swansea had asked children to write in with their requests for favourite items, and soon all regional stations had request weeks, usually two each year. The Children's Hour staff were able to assess the popularity of the year's varied programmes from the thousands of letters which faithfully arrived before each request week. In the 1920s musical items were usually the most popular, with stories second and plays a close third. In the requests of 1932, stories and dialogue stories came out on top with music also high in the requests. Fourth on the list were talks, and this drew the comment in a BBC memorandum 'I think this most gratifying'.

After feature programmes such as Mabel Constanduros' *Buggins Family*, plays and parties came, last of all, verse. This drew the comment in the same memo: 'unfortunately'. Certain items became regular favourites, the outstanding example being the Toytown stories of S. G. Hulme Beaman, which went to the top of the lists almost immediately and stayed there for thirty years. In 1936 the Zoo Man, David Seth-Smith, was second to *Toytown*, closely followed by Stephen King-Hall, *Castles of England* (plays by L. du Garde Peach), *Mary Plain* (stories for younger children), *Worzel Gummidge*, *The Star Gazer*, a play called *Adventurous Journey*, Ronald Gourley (the blind pianist), and *Black Beauty*.

Although much care was now being taken over the planning of the daily Hour, and Arthur Burrows had said 'there is no section of our programme work upon which more time and thought is spent than that termed Children's Hour', not all correspondence was favourable. Criticisms ranged from the view that the programmes were making children passive and all alike, to the commonly held belief that it stopped them from reading books; others argued that it would provide children with a new source of daily satisfaction. The dangers of addiction (such as were later to be levelled at television) were seldom voiced. Instead it was asked, would children get so involved with this fantasy of the air waves that they would not enjoy the real world about them?

In fact, many of the programmes had just the opposite effect. Many tended to extol the virtues of the countryside, nature, science and hobbies, and encouraged the child to investigate the world for him- or herself. The argument of falling book sales was soon shown to be false. The Children's Hour itself gave rise to numerous publications which were directly and indirectly linked to its programmes.

Even Uncle Caractacus' signing-off message, in which he wished his listeners 'pleasant dreams and a hot bath', was criticised on the grounds that at that time many of the poorer families had no bath. Caractacus was not repentant, however, and continued to use the phrase.

Children's Hour Annuals were produced in the very early years of broadcasting. In the 1928 *Annual*, C. E. Hodges (Uncle Peter) tells in his article 'How it is Done' of some disasters to befall presenters. Attempting to make sound effects of water, a presenter placed two bucketfuls directly in front of the actors. As was bound to happen, one of them put their foot in a bucket and the rest of the play was acted out with the studio swimming in water and the players, between lines, trying to mop up the deluge.

— *tut, tut!*

In the middle of another musical play, the lights failed. After an awkward pause the cast scurried in various directions, one searching for matches while another found the microphone and explained what had happened. One aunt had rushed off and found a poetry book, and an impromptu poetry reading session was held by matchlight. Frantic plans were made about what to put on next, but luckily after a few minutes the lights returned, and the original musical entertainment was resumed.

Until 1937 the broadcasts had invariably been on a regional basis, with little or no interchange of programmes except for the Sunday programmes. In 1937 London and the regions began regular interchange with simultaneous broadcasts, and this was improved upon in subsequent years. The adolescent child had hitherto been somewhat neglected, but in 1938 the Under Twenty Club was initiated. The chairman of the club was Howard Marshall, and once a week members discussed various matters with visiting experts. One of the early guests was Sir Malcolm Campbell, speaking on adventure.

4
Household Names

In the forty-two years of Children's Hour, numerous characters emerged to delight their young audience. Following the very first uncles and aunts who pioneered this service came others who built up a faithful following and in so doing became household names.

Derek McCulloch, OBE (Uncle Mac)

Uncle Mac held on to his 'undignified' title throughout his broadcasting career which began, for children, in 1929. He was born in Plymouth on 18 November 1897, and joined the BBC as an announcer when he was thirty-one, after having been badly wounded in the First World War. He left Savoy Hill (the London studios) for a short spell in Belfast, but returned the same year and joined a team organising the London Children's Hour on 1 January 1930. He had lost an eye, a leg and a lung, and sometimes suffered great pain. His career was punctuated by many periods of convalescence, often after operations. These setbacks were not obvious from his warm, friendly manner on the air.

By all reports he was a rather unbending Head of Children's Broadcasting – a post he attained in November 1933. He had quite rigid opinions on some matters and, for example, took a little persuading to broadcast nationally the Romany talks, which had been successful in the North. Perhaps he felt Romany was encroaching on his own field, as he too was a nature lover, and as well as giving outside broadcasts was chairman of the Nature Parliament programmes. (These popular programmes relied also on the talents of such experts as L. Hugh Newman, Peter Scott and Brian Vesey-Fitzgerald.)

Uncle Mac sometimes appeared on other adult programmes. In July 1933 he appeared in John Watt's experimental news/comment programme, when he talked poignantly about the anniversary of the Battle of the Somme. But he was perhaps best known for his portrayal of Larry the Lamb in the Toytown stories, with an inimitable vibrato voice. The Toytown series was dear to his heart, and when Cecil Madden wanted to televise the shows Mac wrote to ask him to ensure that they were given special treatment and that the voice characterisations the children had grown to love were not changed.

Two important people in the story of children's broadcasting: May E. Jenkin (Elizabeth) and Derek McCulloch (Uncle Mac), her predecessor as Director of Children's Hour.

It was he who introduced a signature tune to the Hour in 1934, using an old musical box. Under his direction the programmes reached perhaps their largest audience. He took Children's Hour through the Second World War, and wrote in the *BBC Handbook* of 1945 that in those troubled times the aims of the staff had been to give children a sense of continuity in a world of chaos, and to give them only the best in music, story and drama.

Uncle Mac endeared himself to children by his attitudes on many matters, for example his siding with the 'no homework lobby' when an argument blew up in the Press in 1935. It was thus a sad day for all children when he left in 1951. His broadcasts were not over, however, as he was invited by the Light Programme to host a Children's Favourites request show, which still continues, with a different host, to this day.

Derek McCulloch wrote in an article in *Radio Times* in 1937: 'It is my belief that in providing radio entertainment for children we attempt to crack the hardest nut in all broadcasting; but I do not agree that the solution lies in providing entirely what adults – so often childless adults – believe to be good for children, rather than what children themselves say they prefer.'

Very reasonably, he commented in 1944 that he believed he knew more about children's broadcasting than anyone in the Corporation. Certainly no-one believed more in the vital need for such a service than he did.

It was Mac who coined the phrase 'Goodnight children . . . everywhere', and he ensured that he alone used it. The phrase became especially poignant in the war, when many children were evacuated; in one letter a young girl expressed what many must have felt when she wrote that she knew when Mac said 'everywhere' it meant she wasn't forgotten.

Derek McCulloch died in 1967.

Reverend G. Bramwell Evens (Romany)

Romany's grandfather, Cornelius Smith, had been a wandering gipsy. He was converted to Christianity at a revival meeting, and began himself to convert other gipsies to the faith. The family became friends with the relatives of the founder of the Salvation Army (Bramwell Booth), and that is why Romany was christened Bramwell. He inherited his love of music from his grandfather, who played the violin, but his love of nature and animals was not a gipsy trait and developed throughout his childhood, encouraged by his parents and teachers.

The young Bramwell became used to standing with his parents on evangelist platforms and was always confident in public. He was a divinity student at Queen's College, Taunton, and studied at the Wesleyan Theological College, Handsworth. He was ordained in 1908 and began preaching all over the country, learning more about the countryside as he travelled. In 1921 he bought a caravan, or *vardo* as it is called in Romany, which was to become an important part of his radio programmes. He became an avid photographer, and always took his camera on his numerous excursions.

One afternoon, while walking down Market Street in Manchester, he met someone who, recognising him and knowing of his love of nature and ability to talk in public, said that he was just the man that the Children's Hour in Manchester was looking for. He had already given some talks for schools on the radio and was very interested in the idea. His name was mentioned to Olive Schill, the Manchester organiser, and after an audition he was engaged to take part in the programmes the following month.

He did not want to be called Uncle Bramwell or the Reverend Bramwell Evens. On the spur of the moment he said 'Romany'. It was on 7 October 1932 that *Radio Times* announced, 'We meet the Romany, and learn all about the gipsy trail'. Other northern favourites, the Kookaburra and Rosemary stories, alternated with his talks. In the studio for the first programme were Muriel Levy, Doris Gambell, Eric Fogg and Harry Hopewell. It consisted of Romany telling two stories. Eric Fogg interspersed his usual joviality and Muriel and Doris joined in with 'impromptu fun'. Romany was left at the microphone alone for a few minutes to tell his tales.

It was several months before the talks became a whole half-hour ramble, with Muriel and Doris asking questions, often unscripted, and Romany giving equally unscripted answers. Frank Nichols had been an established favourite as Adam the Gamekeeper, and for several months Romany was introduced only occasionally. Soon, however, with the addition of sound effects and Romany's vivid descriptions, the programmes developed an open-air feeling, and many listeners fully believed that all the action took place outside the studio.

By the time Olive Shapley became the Manchester Children's Hour organiser in 1934, the *Out With Romany* programmes were the most popular in the request weeks. It was about this time that Eric Fogg left the region to become conductor of the Empire Orchestra in London. The programmes were becoming more and more professionally produced, with Terry Cox and Jack Hollinshead taking great pains to get just the right sound effect to fit the action.

Another member of the team in his way as popular as Romany himself was the cocker spaniel Raq. He went on lecture tours with Romany and was almost always present in the studio for the broadcasts. Nan Mcdonald took over as producer of the programme in 1937, and it was in the following year that *Out With Romany* was heard nationally in the scheme started for simultaneous broadcasts from different regions.

It was his love of nature, his vast knowledge of the subject, his spontaneous approach and microphone technique, combined with the talents of Muriel and Doris, that made the programme first a local, then a national, favourite.

Although the programmes were by then carefully scripted and timed, Romany often strayed from the scripted path and Nan Mcdonald would have to put him right by moving the microphone in front of him as he moved about the studio. The programmes were faded out and in to enhance the effect of going out of the studio. There was no intention to deceive listeners, but a silly storm blew up when *Radio Times* published an article telling listeners how it was all done. Shortly afterwards (on 20 November 1943) Romany died, and the shock nationally to children and adults alike was enormous. Some school classes had to be cancelled the following day because children were inconsolable. The condolences and appreciations flooded in to the BBC. Children wrote to make sure Raq was not left alone in the caravan, and the country mourned one of its best-loved personalities. On the anniversary of his death a memorial service was broadcast, and one of the few recordings made of his programmes was repeated.

May E. Jenkin (Elizabeth)

'Elizabeth' took charge of Children's Hour after Mac left, and before W. E. (David) Davis became Head in 1953. Her history with the service dated back to 1927 when, intending to look for a job as a linguist with the League of Nations, she received a letter from the BBC asking her to take charge of the Children's Hour in Newcastle. She had studied languages at Oxford and during the war worked for the Admiralty. While at Oxford she developed a great love for music and the theatre, and the amateur acting she had done stood her in good stead for her work in Newcastle.

She moved to London after only two years and began to be heard in the Hour in plays and in the early zoo programmes. These were accomplished by positioning microphones in different cages throughout the zoo; the aunts and uncles ran from cage to cage, where the keepers tried to coax their animals to perform for the panting announcers.

It was Elizabeth who was responsible for bringing to the air the characters of Larry the Lamb, Ernest the Policeman, Dennis the Dachshund, the Mayors of Toytown and Arkville, and many more, for it was she who discovered the book called *Tales of Toytown* by S. G. Hulme Beaman. She came across it in a shop in 1929 and dramatised a story from it called 'Proud Punch'. The play was immediately popular, further adaptations were made, and the author was asked to write more stories especially for the air.

May Jenkin became Head in 1951, passing the reins to Davis in 1953. She was one of the finest producers and adapters to work on children's programmes, and was made an MBE in the 1945 Birthday Honours. David Davis wrote of her, 'To her colleagues in broadcasting she is the wise and kindly chief for whom no little personal trouble or problem is too much.' She herself once wrote about the secrets of a successful broadcaster: 'Simplicity, sincerity, a sense of humour, friendliness – all these help, but it is charm that succeeds.'

W. E. (David) Davis

'David' is another of the band of people who have dedicated much of their lives to the entertainment and education of children. W. E. Davis studied the classics and French at Oxford, but had been playing the piano from the age of six, and continued his musical studies after he left Oxford and began teaching in Harrogate. He had met a young lady who worked on the London Children's Hour and who was the niece of his headmaster. When she learnt the BBC were having some difficulty in finding an accompanist for the service she wrote and told her uncle, and Davis' attention was drawn to the notice in *The Listener*. He auditioned, got the job and, to complete the story neatly, married the young lady.

As with most members of the staff, David soon became an allrounder. He played and wrote music, introduced, presented record programmes, produced and directed plays and did what he is best remembered for: reading stories. His warm clear voice was as distinctive as it was attractive.

From the beginning those learning to play the piano were not forgotten, and in his regular gramophone recitals on Fridays he included many examination pieces. Musical appreciation was subtly developed in young listeners by the use of light classical music as incidental music and signature tunes for plays and serials. In a recent article in *The Listener*, Roy Hattersley

In 1958 the Children's Hour team celebrated twenty-one years of Regional Round *– the first quiz programme. On left: Josephine Plummer, Assistant Head of Children's Hour; centre: W. E. (David) Davis, Head of Children's Hour; on right: Geoffrey Dearmer, long-serving producer.*

remarked how the music could change from Noël Coward one minute to Vaughan Williams the next, and 'The Wasps Overture' had remained with him as heralding the historical plays of L. du Garde Peach.

The dramatic productions during Davis' period with the Hour were of the highest standard – often with very short rehearsal time, but planned with meticulous efficiency. *Box of Delights*, *Eagle of the Ninth* and *Ballet Shoes* are just three of the notable productions for which he was responsible. By the time he became organiser much use was being made of productions from other regions which could be linked into the national programme.

This arrangement started before the Second World War, and provided a pool of material often of excellent quality because each regional team could spend more time on its individual productions.

Davis had the task of planning his quarterly schedules, having received lists of the new productions from each region for the coming months. Occasionally, when programmes were running short, it was necessary to fill in with gramophone records; this happened on one occasion when the studio was being visited by Princesses Elizabeth and Margaret and their mother. Davis, having had prior warning of the visit, was able to fill in with 'The Queen's Jig' and, looking up at the gallery, was rewarded with a warm smile. It was also Davis who produced the Jennings serials written by Anthony Buckeridge and starring Glyn Dearman.

His attitude towards children, like that of most of his contemporaries, was to treat them (in his own phrase) as 'co-equals', and the style did not change with the age group of the listener – only the material. It was sad that a man who had 'sown seeds and opened windows for generations' was to see the end of Children's Hour. The audiences had diminished with the coming of BBC TV and later of commercial television and, as explained in greater detail later, it was decided that this national institution, which had won world acclaim, should be taken off the air.

Stephen King-Hall

Commander, later Sir, Stephen King-Hall began his talks for children on 17 October 1930. 'Steve's' father and uncle were both admirals, as was his grandfather. He himself fought in HMS *Southampton* at Jutland. He was born in 1893 and, not surprisingly with his ancestry, went into the armed forces. He taught at the Army Staff College and served as Intelligence Officer with the Mediterranean Fleet. In 1929 he joined the staff of the Royal Institute for International Affairs. He was asked by the BBC if he would give a series of talks on the political side of the news.

Mac was, by this time, presenting a weekly news item, but the staff's background knowledge was limited and Steve's experience on national and international politics was vast. He had written *Western Civilisation and the Far East* and other non-fiction as well as children's books – *Letters to Hilary* and *Hilary Growing Up* – and was a great find for the BBC as he was able to

Commander Stephen King-Hall at the microphone. Known to millions as 'Steve', he simultaneously held a government post while regularly broadcasting on Children's Hour and on the Empire (short wave) transmissions to Australia, New Zealand, South Africa and North America. These weekly wartime broadcasts went under the title Hello Children *and were an attempt to relieve the anxiety felt by those who had been evacuated.*

explain complex political matters simply and had a warm microphone manner.

It was realised that this was to be an important innovation, and the extra money for it was eventually found. As well as giving his talks under the heading *Here and There*, he began to write articles for children in *Radio Times* called 'There and Here'. In the edition for 9 July 1937 he wrote a letter to all his listeners saying goodbye, and telling them that his last talk was to be that week. In the letter he recalled the time a mother had brought her paralysed child to meet him and said to him, 'For five years you have been his window on life.' Steve commented: 'I felt, as I never had before, the terrifying responsibility of working for the BBC. One feels that it is more than anyone should attempt to carry on for too long a period . . . Goodbye children, and thank you very much for listening so patiently for so many years.'

That last talk was his 290th, and he had broadcast every week since October 1930 except when abroad. At the end of the broadcast he left his audience with his now famous sign-off line: 'Be good. But not so frightfully good that someone says to you, "Ah! and what mischief are you up to?" So if I were you I should be just fairly good.'

How could he not endear himself to children with remarks like that? He could not stay away for long, and returned in April to give another talk and an occasional series continued under the new heading *Here and Thereabouts*. In the war he gave world affairs talks, sometimes clashing with Mac who thought war news should be kept to a minimum. He also told *Stories from Hansard* some years later. Stephen King-Hall made his television début in 1938 in *Speaking Personally*, thereafter appearing regularly in magazine programmes such as *Focus*, with his topical commentaries interspersed with anecdotes in an unchanging knowledgeable but friendly style.

David Seth-Smith

Seth-Smith gained great popularity as the Children's Hour Zoo Man, beginning his animal talks in January 1934. He was an immediate success, and was always in the top three or four in the request week polls. He was born in the heart of the countryside, and it is said that his first word was not mummy or daddy but 'owlie'!

Although he studied civil engineering and architecture, David's great love of animals and the countryside led him to become a member of the Royal Zoological Society of London. He began by keeping his own birds and eventually became Curator of Birds and later of Birds and Mammals, being invited to serve as a member of the Society's council. Derek McCulloch persuaded him to become one of the Children's Hour experts, and as the Zoo Man he broadcast regularly in the thirties and forties. He also appeared on television in *Friends from the Zoos*, beginning in 1937, and was the first to be asked to contribute to the *Radio Times* Children's Page.

Animals have always been a special love of children, and several broadcasters have concentrated on this sure-fire topic. Zoo programmes had been heard as early as 1924, and in April 1929 the 100th zoo programme was broadcast. It was Leslie Mainland (L.G.M. of the *Daily Mail*) who became the first to specialise in giving talks on animals, on the London and Daventry stations. Mainland had an endearing personality and, with his catchphrases 'Zoo stories are true stories' and 'Well, it's a hard life children. Goodbye and good luck to you', became a firm favourite until his death in June 1930.

Seth-Smith became Mainland's successor in the South, while in Scotland H. Mortimer Batten broadcast stories about wild animals. In the North of England Bertram Miles, a lecturer in zoology at Manchester University, gave some animal talks, and Gerald Iles, who began his talks in 1944, became a popular northern broadcaster on both radio and television. He was a keeper at Belle Vue Zoo in the centre of Manchester and occasionally brought animals into the studio when giving talks.

In the Midlands the regional expert was Gladys Davidson, who gave talks about Whipsnade Zoo and other nature topics. B.K. Vallings, better known to listeners as 'Snowshoe', spoke about the great outdoors of Canada (where he had lived on ranches), while Olive Huntley was the Birmingham station's answer to Percy Edwards. Henry Williamson, the author, gave some nature talks under the title *Walks with my Children* from the West of England studio. Yet another Zoo Man was Craven Hill, who broadcast and also contributed to the Children's Page in *Radio Times*. When Romany died he had several successors. One who became well known was 'Nomad'. Walking and talking became a favourite theme on many stations. Even Wilfred Pickles broadcast regular treks from the North.

Great attempts were made to take the listeners out of their sitting-rooms and into the countryside and garden. C. H. Middleton, the well-known gardener, gave a series of talks on Children's Hour in 1934. He also provided *Radio Times* with many articles for the Children's Page. Middleton's father had been a gardener, and he followed in his father's bootprints, working at Kew Gardens and later becoming an inspector at the Ministry of Agriculture.

Middleton worked for the Surrey County Council on their horticultural advisory staff, and began a long broadcasting career in 1931, becoming the BBC's resident gardener. A gate dedicated to his memory stands at the entrance to the small garden between 10 and 12 Cavendish Place in London.

Fred Loads, during twenty years of gardening programmes for children in the North Region, was often joined by Violet Carson and Doris Gambell – who asked the occasional gardening question but more frequently ended the programme with an appropriate song. Percy Thrower began a series of ten-minute gardening talks for the Midland Region in February 1950 called *Our Garden*. It was produced by Peggy Bacon, and its aim was not only to encourage an interest in gardening but also to discourage vandalism in the parks. Percy visited several parks where children had plots. An annual flower show was arranged, with prizes awarded for the best blooms.

John Morgan, who had been a farm labourer, eventually owned his own farm in Sussex and became 'The Farmer' on London Children's Hour. He broadcast numerous talks about the outdoor life, as did the appropriately named Jim Farmer, his contemporary on the Welsh station.

The beauty of nature and the inherent nobility of animals was a constant theme in the nature programmes. It can be best illustrated by a memo written by David Davis in 1954. There had been a suggestion that the

Children's Hour should broadcast a circus, but in a note to his superiors Davis wrote that the policy of the Hour, set out long before, was based on the philosophy that as an animal is one of God's creatures it was therefore worthy of respect. It went on: 'The acts, in cages, are contrary to the natural behaviour of animals, which is held in high esteem in other Children's Hour programmes.' This attitude was questioned by Michael Standing, and certainly television did not seem to have such scruples.

When the Ministry of Agriculture issued a directive to destroy the nests of house-sparrows, which they said were devouring crops, Mac ensured that no mention of it should be heard on the Hour. In fact he proposed to counter, with Seth-Smith giving a talk on the good that birds do. The Hour's attitude – to uplift rather than degrade – pervaded its whole make-up and was one of its greatest strengths.

Vernon Bartlett

Born in 1894, Bartlett was both a novelist and an expert on international affairs. From 1922 to 1932 he was Director of the League of Nations Secretariat. He wrote a series of short stories called *Topsy-Turvy* and several novels, and in August 1927 made his first broadcast for the BBC. His background experience had been gleaned from travels in Germany, Italy, Spain and France, where he went immediately after leaving school. He had served in the First World War, but had been invalided out, and after two years of severe illness went into journalism, working for the *Daily Mail*, Reuters and the *Daily Herald*. He later gained more experience of Europe while reporting for *The Times* and, most notably, for the *News Chronicle*.

In January 1928, Bartlett began a series of talks for Children's Hour called *The Way of The World*. These continued for several years, as did his broadcasts for the BBC's Home and External Services.

Ralph de Rohan

Born in London in 1877, de Rohan did not begin broadcasting – in his distinctive way – until 1925. He made a name as 'The Wicked Uncle' or more tersely 'Wunkle', with a style of surrealistic imagination resembling that of Edward Lear or Spike Milligan. He derived his name from one of his first broadcasts when he became the wicked uncle of the Babes in the Wood. He was often to be heard reciting one of his 'poetries' or telling one of his fantastic tales. His mythical home was Folly Manor, Little Lamb Green, where he invented impossible machines and read his 'book of magic'. De Rohan's voice may be remembered as Mr Growser in some of the very early Toytown productions in London. He was not on the staff of the BBC, and some idea of the fees paid for freelance services on Children's Hour at that time can be illustrated by the increase in March 1929 of his session fee from two to *three* guineas!

*Helping the magic of Toytown to span the years. Above: Felix Felton,
Philip Wade, Ivan Samson, Freddie Burtwell, Ralph de Rohan – 1941;
below: Ivan Samson (again), Ernest Jay, Norman Shelley – 1952.*

Norman Shelley

Born in 1903, Norman Shelley originally intended to work as an aircraft designer, but after developing an interest in acting and gaining some experience on the stage he made his first broadcast for the BBC in 1926. He was notable as the man who recorded one of Churchill's most famous wartime speeches, which was sent for broadcasting in America.

But he became even better known for a very different role – that of A. A. Milne's immortal honey-loving bear, Winnie the Pooh. Shelley *was* Pooh, and millions could accept no other once they had heard him. His voice, his interpretation, his singing cannot be improved upon. He was also Dennis the Dachshund in some of the Toytown plays, and at one time was regularly appearing in radio plays each week. He took many roles both serious and lighthearted, and may be remembered by another generation of children in the fifties as the 'old gentleman' in the first television adaptation of E. Nesbit's *The Railway Children*.

Richard Goolden

After showing acting ability at Oxford and then Army duty, Richard Goolden made his first stage appearance in London in 1925. His radio début had been two years earlier when, as an undergraduate, he was given the job of interrupting a late-night dance programme with wisecracks.

He became famous for a totally different style of humour in the role of Mole. He had been given small parts on the London station until in 1930 he appeared as Mole in Kenneth Grahame's *Toad of Toad Hall* at the Lyric Theatre. When the play was performed on Children's Hour he was offered the Mole part, and played it again in *The Wind in the Willows*. The rest is theatrical legend, Goolden having played the role annually until the age of eighty-four.

Goolden also became famous for the role of Mr Penny on the stage, in the film *Meet Mr Penny* and in a series of lighthearted radio plays, and acted in numerous other radio plays including the children's broadcasts of the Roads of England and Waterways of England plays by L. du Garde Peach. To Mac he was always 'the funny little man', but to children he was only one character and they even wrote letters to 'Mr Mole, Children's Hour, London'.

Also part of the broadcasting story . . .

One man who made his name as an actor in Children's Hour and then changed it was Lionel Gamlin, who originally appeared as Lionel James. He later presented holiday programmes which had a large juvenile audience. He became one of the presenters of *In Town Tonight*, *Puzzle Corner* and *Music Hall*.

Felix Felton – writer, director and actor – was another stalwart of London Children's Hour. He was born in 1914 and went straight into the BBC after studying at Balliol College, Oxford. On the Hour he was perhaps most often heard as the Mayor in the Toytown series, his voice as crisp and chunky as a Cox's apple.

Many other fine actors such as Laidman Browne, Carleton Hobbs, Preston Lockwood, Ralph Truman and Hugh Morton were regulars in plays and dramatised documentaries. Morton was based at the Birmingham station, where he joined the Children's Hour team in 1935. He introduced items and played records as well as being a fine storyteller. When the Paul Temple detective series began, he was given the title role.

All the regions produced their own favourite contributors. Enid Maxwell, at one time in charge of the Birmingham children's programmes, was known as 'Anne'. She had previously worked in Edinburgh under the name of 'Tinker Bell', which she tried to live down for many years. Jack Cowper was 'Jacko', senior announcer in Birmingham in the 1930s and a very popular figure on the children's service.

Victor ('Bunny') Hely-Hutchinson contributed to their programme musically, and became Director of BBC Music. He wrote several children's operettas and was also noted for his beside-the-piano talks. He died at the age of forty-five in 1947. One of the early contributors to the Midlands service was Robert Tredinnick (Uncle Robert). He was famous for his Kate and Henry Lion stories, and was the first to broadcast full-length record recitals to children. He was a prolific story writer, and it is said that over 300 of his stories were told in the twenties and thirties.

Marjorie Westbury was a member of the Midland Singers, and often sang for children as well as acting in many plays. She became 'Steve' in the post-war Paul Temple episodes. Dorothy Summers also appeared in countless plays in the region, but is best remembered for her role as Mrs Mopp in *ITMA*, croaking one of the most famous of wartime phrases, 'Can I do you now, sir?' It was the Birmingham director Percy Edgar who first introduced Adrian Boult to the microphone and he, like Malcolm Sargent, Walford Davies, Edward Clark and Charles Groves, gave regular music recitals and talks for children.

From Bristol, serving the West of England, Hedley Goodall was a regular contributor, taking many character parts in plays and reading stories and poems including a series in West Country dialect. Music was provided by Winifred Davey, Norman Jones and Beryl Tichbon – playing syncopated piano solos; also by Glyn Eastman, Victor Hunt and Mervyn Saunders, and the Bristol Chamber Trio – obviously a station that set great store by music. Barry Kemble and Clifford Hemsley provided light relief with their antics as clowns Bimbo and Koko. Hedley Goodall, as well as appearing in many plays, also trained children to act and developed young talent in Bristol.

Famous names in the North of England included Olive Shapley, who was known to listeners as 'Anna' and promoted many programmes presented by children themselves, whether variety or the Your Own Ideas series. Doris Gambell and Muriel Levy, as well as writing and acting, teamed up with Violet Carson to form the famous Three Semis, giving many sing-alongs and appearing in variety shows such as *Stuff and Nonsense*.

Their *Nursery Sing-Songs* celebrated twenty-one years in 1959. 'Denis

Violet Carson, Doris Gambell, Nan Macdonald, Wilfred Pickles, Muriel Levy – talented performers on the Manchester station. Pickles learned a good deal about the art of broadcasting through reading stories and acting in plays on the Hour. He worked originally as a freelance artist, receiving the customary one guinea (or 'at the most thirty shillings') for each children's programme.

Decibel' on top of Broadcasting House in Manchester must have heard literally hundreds of renderings of tunes like 'Baa Baa Black Sheep', 'The Teddy Bears' Picnic' and 'They're Changing Guard at Buckingham Palace' – the last of these always sounding so much better with drum beats and trumpet calls by Herbert Smith.

Violet Carson, who was to make her international name as Ena Sharples in Granada TV's *Coronation Street*, was born in Ancoats in the centre of Manchester. She had loved music from an early age, and worked as a cinema pianist accompanying silent films. She became an accompanist on the Manchester station, then Auntie Vi on Children's Hour, and featured in the early programmes with Wilfred Pickles. Barney Colehan, the producer of *Have A Go*, was always amazed how, in whatever key the contestants attempted to sing a party piece on the show, she could follow them as if they had rehearsed for hours.

A fourteen-year-old boy, Tony Simpson, met Violet Carson in the BBC studios when they were both to take part in a play called *Secret of Hollow Hill*, and remembered her singing about the occupants of a Manchester back street when the recording link to London was broken, and she sat at the piano entertaining a cast of nervous children. That boy later changed his name to Tony Warren and devised *Coronation Street*, perhaps with that song's memory still in his mind. Violet Carson received an OBE in the 1965 Birthday Honours.

It was not only music for the very young that was heard over the air waves – in fact, children were asked to send in serious pieces of music they had written. Compositions were received from Peter Hodgson, Peter Maxwell Davies and others who have since gone on to greater musical achievements. Performers too were encouraged in such programmes as *First Attempts*, which included young artists from all the regions.

As early as 1929, young Robert Donat read poems such as the 'The Pied Piper' on the Manchester children's programmes. Much later, in 1949, two child actresses appeared in some of their first radio parts on the Hour. These were Judith Chalmers and Billie Whitelaw, two of the many to gain valuable experience from that training ground. The classic Masefield play *Box of Delights*, broadcast from London in 1943, gave John Gilpin his first opportunity to appear on radio. He later took part in the Sunday serial *The Little Stuarts*.

Petula Clark had been heard in *It's All Yours* sending a message to her soldier uncle in Iraq, and sang 'Mighty Like a Rose'. But it was London's Children's Hour which gave her the opportunity to develop her talents. Vanessa and Corin Redgrave also got their first big break in children's plays. Gordon Jackson had his first acting experience on Children's Hour in Scotland.

Much fine drama and light entertainment emanated from the North, with Trevor Hill, Herbert Smith and Nan Macdonald producing and characters such as Frank Nichols, known to thousands of listeners as Harry Hopeful, creating the personalities of Adam the Gamekeeper, Worzel Gummidge, and Mr Dock the Gardener. Noel Morris, another Manchester regular, often played the part of the lugubrious Yorkshire tailor's apprentice in the Jeremiah Merriman series.

The Welsh and West of England stations developed close links, and organised an exchange programme long before that was arranged nationally. Elwyn Evans handled the Cardiff end of the arrangement and adventure stories, outside broadcasts, and talks mainly for older children tended to predominate in that region. Gunstone Jones and Donald Wells became regulars in the roles of Dai and Horace in the adventure plays written by J. D. Strange. Other actors often heard in this region were Tom Jones, Philip and Arthur Phillips, and Lyn Joshua. Alun Oldfield Davies was Cardiff's answer to Stephen King-Hall.

In Aberdeen, where the entertainers chose the most endearing of *noms de plume*, regulars included Ruby Duncan, who was known as 'Squirrel'. She was a pianist, as was Bill Thomson ('Giraffe'). Howard M. Lockhart, who began broadcasting in 1923, became Children's Hour organiser in the 1930s. All the staff were given the names of animals and he was no exception, being called 'Howard the Hare'. Moultrie R. Kelsall was known as 'Brer Rabbit' and Addie Ross was called 'Miss Mouse'.

Edinburgh and Glasgow also provided children's programmes. Glasgow supplied A. K. MacDonald, who gave fortnightly talks on stamp collecting, and W. Kersley Holmes, who organised a regular *Birthday Book* programme and gave talks on rock climbing. Music was contributed by pianist Barbara Laing. Christine Orr and Betty Ogilvy deserve mention for their organisation and presentation of children's programmes in Scotland. *Tammy Troot* and the popular *Down at the Mains* also emanated from the Scottish studios.

Ursula Eason took charge of the Northern Ireland service in 1934 and, among other duties, introduced many music programmes. Later she edited several of the *BBC Children's Annuals* and moved into the children's television service, completing fifty years of entertaining youngsters. Mary Curran was a regular on the Northern Ireland station for many years singing, playing, acting and telling stories. T. O. Corrin (Uncle Tom) told stories of operas, and Jimmy Mageen was as well known on the children's programmes as he was in the evening plays.

The list of artists who contributed to those early years is certainly long, but a few more must be mentioned. Announcers Stuart Hibberd and F. H. Grisewood (Freddie) were often to be heard singing and entertaining children, and Hibberd achieved some fame with his mouth organ, as a member of the 'Toy Band'. He wrote in his diary for 23 December 1937: 'A most enjoyable family party was held in the Children's Hour in a bakingly hot studio in the sub-basement. Mabel Constanduros, as Grandma, introduced each one of us in turn. We had a percussion band, in which I helped to make noises with a mouth organ; there were two pianos and various other noises off. Both Marson (Lionel) and Gamlin (Lionel) were in good form. The *pièce de résistance* was Grandma's story of Alfred and the Cakes . . . I literally ached with laughing.'

'Ajax' was T. C. L. Farrar, who became famous for his readings of the Professor Branestawm stories. It was Norman Hunter who wrote the hilarious adventures of the gadget-inventing professor for radio, and these were later produced in book form. The first collection, *The Incredible Adventures of Professor Branestawm*, was dedicated to Ajax, who had made them so popular. Miss M. Newell was the 'Little Auntie'; Ernest Lush was a notable accompanist; and another musician who gathered a great number of friends through the Hour was the blind pianist Ronald Gourley.

Then there was 'Wonderful James' – no, not another performer, but a pianola taken out of service before the move in 1932 to Broadcasting House – and 'Genial Jemima', a gramophone that did make the move.

The writers were the real miracle-workers of the Children's Hour, for they could bring ancient battles, outer space or the pioneers of the Wild West into your own home. They could, on a cold, dark winter's evening, shroud your bedroom with a shivering ghost story or make you laugh out loud at the antics of Larry the Lamb. They could expand your own imagination, letting you paint an individual picture from the evocative sound.

L. du Garde Peach

The BBC commissioned numerous writers to write specifically for the Children's Hour, and many of the staff contributed plays, stories and poems. But perhaps the most prolific and talented of all was Lawrence du Garde Peach. He was born in Sheffield, where his father was a clergyman, but he spent much of his early life in their country house at Great Hucklow near Buxton. It was there he dreamt up stories about lion-inhabited woods and adventures with pirates, and it was there, some years later, that he was to write plays for the local dramatic society and make both his own and their name famous.

Peach went to Manchester Grammar School, and later attended Manchester and Göttingen universities, obtaining Master of Arts and Doctor of Philosophy degrees. He served in the First World War with the 8th Battalion, Manchester Regiment, and it was at that time that he had his first play, *Winds o' the Moors*, produced by Lewis Casson at the Gaiety Theatre, Manchester, and took a curtain call in khaki uniform.

In 1919 he became a university lecturer. One night, three years later, he looked in at the Manchester station in Trafford Park, where Kenneth Wright was in charge. As some artists were unable to attend (not an uncommon occurrence in those days), he found himself telling stories, singing and generally filling in. This was to be the beginning of a very long association with broadcasting.

Peach's play *Light and Shade* was one of the first plays ever broadcast, and was acted in subdued light to create atmosphere. A series of short radio plays followed, and then he wrote *Ingredient X*, a full-length play – one of the first of its length to be broadcast. He was asked to write for Children's Hour, and out poured a torrent of potted histories under the series titles of *Arthurian Legends, Fables of Aesop, Nordic Sagas, Tower of London, Roads of England, Waterways of England*, and *Castles of England*. The dramatised histories were obviously intended to inspire the young listeners with stories of their heritage. In *Castles of England*, for example, Peach used the device of a herald to set out the historical scene or to sum up events, perhaps with some moral. Sometimes it was up to one of the characters to make a patriotic point. Geoffrey Chaucer, in the play about Windsor Castle, ends the play: 'Yes. Windsor Castle stands for England and the English people; for their pride and their strength, for their faith and their tolerance. It is the symbol of all that is best in our race. May it stand as long as the English race endures.'

L. du Garde Peach – children's playwright par excellence. Something of his style can be gathered from his own brief history, written in 1933. 'Was born in Sheffield, but not recently. This event, the importance of which (to L. du G.) it is impossible to overestimate, happened forty years ago, but is still talked about in Sheffield. After trying whooping cough, measles, and scarlet fever, decided to look elsewhere for a career.'

Peach wrote for *Punch*, where he was able to display his humour, as he did in his infrequent live broadcasts, which had such titles as *Is Chivalry Dead?*, *Swiss Rolls*, and *Easter Eggs I Have Known*. It was the radio play on which, like Cecil Lewis, he concentrated his efforts and for which he is best remembered.

Another playwright who enjoyed the challenge of writing for children was Franklyn Kelsey who, although originally a singer, began writing thrillers for the Hour in 1929 and widened his scope to produce numerous scripts.

When management criticised the standards of Kelsey's adaptation of Haggard's *Children of the Sun*, Derek McCulloch wrote back, pointing out that in the request week letters on that particular series had notched up 3000 votes, and 800 letters had asked for a sequel. Kelsey wrote many equally popular series, including *Southward Ho, Robin Hood, The Shield of Malchus* and *Island of the Mist*.

One of the great success stories of Children's Hour, as already recorded, was the discovery and exploitation of the work of Sidney George Hulme Beaman. The remarkably gifted Beaman was born in Tottenham in 1887. He studied art after school, and embarked on an artistic career by carving children's toys, later turning to drawing. He had his first cartoon published in a local newspaper in 1923. He had several other books published before *The Tales of Toytown* appeared in 1928.

Children's Hour presented the first story in 1929, and Beaman, as well as writing the adaptation, began to produce models of the characters and built up complete Toytown sets. There was a stage production of his work in 1947, and in 1950 the television series began. Beaman was not to see these, as he had died in 1932. By that time, however, he had enriched Children's Hour with some twenty-five plays and three Christmas 'specials'. The first play he wrote especially for the Hour was called aptly *How Wireless Came to Toyland*.

The plays were broadcast regularly, often monthly, until the end of Children's Hour in 1964. With the regions producing their own programmes in the thirties, it was not unusual to see two or three different Toytown productions with different casts in the same week, such was their popularity.

Victor Hely-Hutchinson first broadcast on the London Children's Hour in 1926. A talented musician, he became one of the prominent contributors to the Midland station, and with L. du Garde Peach wrote *Hearts are Trumps, The Sand Castles*, and *The Charcoal Burner's Son* – all popular operettas, the last of them later being produced for adult listeners. He also gave talks entitled *Great Composers and the Piano*. Mary Richards was another prolific writer for the Midland station, beginning in 1929 with *When Father Christmas Calls*.

J. D. Strange wrote many serialised plays for the Welsh Region, including *The Man from Mars, The Lost City, Forgotten Island*, and *The*

THE CHILDREN'S HOUR programmes

877 kc/s **REGIONAL** 342.1 m.

5.0 A TOYTOWN DIALOGUE
STORY
by S. G. Hulme-Beaman
' The Showing Up of Larry the
Lamb '
Despite the ' showing up ', Larry
emerges on top, as usual

5.35   A Pianoforte Interlude

5.45   THE ZOO MAN

1013 kc/s   **MIDLAND**   296.2 m.
5.0-6.0   Regional Programme

668 kc/s   **NORTH**   449.1 m.
5.0   Regional Programme

At 5.0 this afternoon children are to hear the story of ' The Showing Up of
Larry the Lamb '. Note how sorry Larry looks!

Toytown brought to life by S. G. Hulme Beaman in the pages of Radio
Times (*18 December 1931 and 14 February 1938*).

Mandarin's Coat. These serials became so popular in Wales, it was said that people left work early in order to be home in time to hear them.

Olive Dehn provided much material for the North Region, as did Sybil Clarke with her Georgina Pauline stories and Catherine Buckle, author of the Jeremiah Merriman series. Muriel Levy, who began her radio career in Liverpool, wrote and adapted numerous plays, especially during her long association with the Manchester studios. Among her many excellent adaptations were *The Jackdaw of Rheims* and the first radio adaptation of Galsworthy's *The Forsyte Saga*.

Children were often indebted to Children's Hour for providing their first encounter with the classics of Dickens, Defoe, Scott, Stevenson and Thackeray. Some of the most popular serialisations were of children's classics: *The Wind in the Willows* by Kenneth Grahame, *Alice in Wonderland* and *Through The Looking Glass* by Lewis Carroll, Charles Kingsley's *The Water Babies*, and the ever popular *Just So Stories* by Rudyard Kipling. *Cowleaze Farm* by Ralph Whitelock, the intrigues of Norman and Henry Bones written by Anthony Wilson, and the exciting original stories by Angus McVicar are just three examples of later drama especially written or adapted for the Hour. Another popular series of plays were those written by Anthony Buckeridge, himself a schoolmaster, about the adventures of an 'eager, friendly boy . . . with untidy brown hair', namely Jennings. Jennings never deliberately caused trouble, but he caused it nevertheless,

Mac reads a Mortimer Batten story while some regions decide to slip in their own items before the broadcast of the play The Secret Garden, *which all areas take. With programming organised in this way the regions could provide items of local interest while still being able to switch into the national network when they wished* (Radio Times 5 October 1938).

HE CHILDREN'S HOUR· programmes for all Regions 5.0—6.0

RUFF. Mac will continue his reading of Mortimer Batten's life story of a fox this afternoon at 5.0.

877 kc/s **REGIONAL** 342.1 m.
1013 kc/s **MIDLAND** 296.2 m.
804 kc/s **WALES** 373.1 m.
977 kc/s **N. IRELAND** 307.1 m.
5.0 Mac will continue the story of
'RED RUFF'
by Mortimer Batten
(From Regional).

5.15 'THE SECRET GARDEN'
A play by Olive Dehn based on the story by Frances Hodgson Burnett
The cast includes Barbara Rumsey, Ian Miller, Charles Lefeaux, Dora Gregory, Audrey Cameron, Charles Hawtrey, and Philip Wade
This is a story by the author of 'Little Lord Fauntleroy', adapted for broadcasting by Olive Dehn. Olive Dehn is particularly well known to Northern listeners and has written a great many stories and poems for the Children's Hour. 'The Secret

Garden' tells of a lonely little girl who, after losing her parents in India, is sent to live in a big gloomy house in Yorkshire. Near the house she discovers an old walled garden and, through making him share her love of it, she succeeds in winning back to health a poor little cripple boy whom she finds living in the house. 'The Secret Garden' was first broadcast in the North some years ago and was heard by London listeners in February last year.
(From Regional)

668 kc/s **NORTH** 449.1 m.
5.0 A MUSICAL COMPETITION
5.15 Regional Programme

767 kc/s **SCOTTISH** 391.1 m.
5.0 'FIVE O'CLOCK FARE'
A programme of gramophone records for the very youngest listeners
5.15 Regional Programme

usually exclaiming, 'Gosh, fish-hooks!' as he realised the predicament he was in. Darbishire, his school chum and a perfect foil for him, was politeness itself and never wanted to get mixed up with the trouble Jennings always managed to get them into.

In 1947 Noel Streatfeild was invited to adapt her *Ballet Shoes* for Children's Hour. The play was produced again in 1948, in 1950, and in 1956 with its hypnotic theme music of 'The Jewel Song' from *The Madonna* by Wolf-Ferrari. Noel visited the BBC studios to watch the first production, and was so stimulated by the quality of the radio drama that she went on to write a succession of plays, including the famous Bell Family stories.

No one was more strongly devoted to the juvenile audience than Arthur Davenport who wrote, among other items, the popular *Country Holiday* dialogue stories featuring Anthony and Noel. When he died in 1934, it was realised that he had written the last stories in much pain, and in fact an unfinished manuscript of his next children's play lay at his bedside.

5

Growth and Decline

By the mid-thirties the Children's Hour was a national institution. It was said that radio only produced two art forms of its own: radio drama and Children's Hour. In London, the request weeks stimulated over 50,000 children to write in with their favourites, and each year the appeals provided increasing donations to charities.

Occasionally, when the regions produced a special programme, a spectacular variety from Glasgow or a 'Goodwill Day' programme from the West Region, this was relayed nationally. This was to occur increasingly with the changes in transmissions in 1934. In September of that year output from the new Droitwich transmitter was established, and the alteration of areas necessitated changes in the distribution of the children's programmes.

Some were forced to lose old friends, and Mac for one was upset by the arrangements. The changes also meant that on Saturdays there was a regular exchange of programmes, with a rota of stations providing entertainment on that day. There were some other innovations. A series of word-pictures of European cities was broadcast, with people from the different nations featured in an attempt to stimulate a friendly interchange of interest.

In July 1935 the Children's Hour was grouped under the control of the Drama department with Val Gielgud at its head. Gielgud had plans for the Hour, some of which were not readily accepted. In 1937 he was reported in the Press as feeling that the Children's Hour should become more formalised. He argued that with plays, as with music, the standard need not be lowered for children.

In response, Frank Kelsey wrote in *Radio Times* (16 April) that, although he agreed that music could be enjoyed by young and old alike, a child did not always have sufficient experience to understand and assimilate all that some radio plays contained.

In fact he thought a 'better' play could easily 'subtract' from their enjoyment and education. He also utterly rejected the formalising of the broadcasts, saying that 'children detest formality, to them it is hollow and pretentious'. He concluded: 'In the child's appreciation of a direct, personal

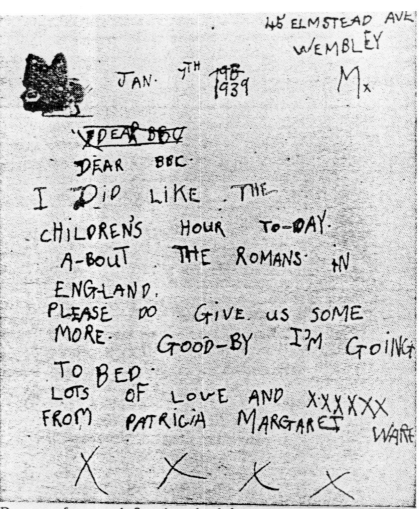

Between four and five hundred letters a month arrive at the BBC from Children's Hour listeners—and here is one, typical of many.

'Dear BBC . . .' The caption to this letter says it all (Radio Times 27 *January 1939*).

and friendly approach, in its love of unaffected simplicity, and above all, in the unconscious influence which may be exerted on its character by voices it knows and trusts, the British Broadcasting Corporation holds in its charge a jewel of great price. To cast aside such richness for the shadow of a sterile formalism, or impersonal mechanisms would, I believe, be nothing less than a tragedy.'

Children's Hour was essentially a two-way service: Radio Times *provided a useful back-up in the days before television. Other papers such as the* Radio Pictorial *also carried weekly articles linked with Children's Hour* (Radio Times *5 July 1935*).

Gielgud was forced to reply to this eloquent plea, and denied that he was going to 'dignify' the programmes or change their personal friendly nature, but he wanted to get away from the 'auntie' image and such utterances as 'kiddiwinkies', which he claimed treated children as morons. He reiterated that he wanted to use good quality work, but that was not to say it would be dreary or intellectual. He felt that children need not always be surrounded by aunts and uncles, but could occasionally benefit from the company of a visitor who treated them as equals. Basically, he wished to broaden the child's outlook. His influence, however, was not to last much longer, for in March 1938 Children's Hour regained its 'independence'.

By the beginning of the war, over four million children (and probably as many adults) listened regularly to the Hour. In early September 1939 its staff, along with those of Variety, Religion and the BBC Orchestra, moved to Bristol, and because of the confinement of these departments a far closer relationship developed.

There was a four-day break in children's programmes, but from 6 September they were back in business if only with a half-hour transmission. It was policy at the start of the Bristol service to restrict all programmes to thirty minutes. Postal competitions were stopped so as not to burden the Post Office.

By the end of 1939 the team was well established and was drawing on material from Scotland, the North, West of England and Wales. Top-level discussion about programmes led to a decision to present old favourites to reassure the listeners, while necessarily involving some new material from the regions. The normal quarterly planning scheme had to be dropped in the new situation, and Mac had to put up with a weekly 'hand-to-mouth' plan. He found this most unsatisfactory, as he often had to decide which programmes to use without full information and scripts in front of him. He began to feel that the standard of programmes was dropping, and he was especially critical of some regional contributions.

In these last months of 1939 the mix of programmes included only one or two each week from the regions, and much correspondence dealt with the irritation the regions felt about lack of air time. Mac, however, was adamant that the brief synopses of proposed programmes which the regions sent him were not sufficient for him to judge a programme's worth, and he also felt his voice and that of May Jenkin should be heard a good deal in the turmoil of the first few months of war.

Mac had an added difficulty when dealing with the regions in that the Children's Hour was designated a section rather than a department, and the regional teams dealing with children's programmes were responsible to their own regional department. His position and authority were, therefore, ill defined. Nevertheless, programmes still managed to get on the air and the only disorganisation obvious to the listener was the occasional break in transmission when a line from one of the regions failed. The few gaps were speedily filled with records.

In a policy document written in 1942 Mac laid down some objectives which, among other things, mentioned the need to aid the moral and religious education of children. Close links had developed with the Religious department, and this had given rise to a new Sunday Children's Hour. Mac, May Jenkin, Dr J. W. Welch (Director of Religious Broadcasting) and his assistant Geoffrey Dearmer had collaborated in these Sunday programmes, which had begun in October 1939.

There was pressure to increase the duration of the broadcasts, and eventually forty-five-minute programmes of plays, music and poetry could be heard on Sunday as well as the rest of the week. The new Sunday shows

THAT

MOBILE X-RAY
UNIT

By Derek McCulloch
Children's Hour Director

THIS is the story of how £1,500 became £15,000. In November last it was with some trepidation that I launched the Children's Hour Appeal. Usually it is for Christmas comforts for poorer children, but in wartime we foresaw all kinds of difficulties, particularly because so many children are evacuated. My first wartime appeal, in November 1939, was for children's hospitals, and here again we feared a poor result. Oddly enough, a record total was received over all other Children's Hour Appeals. It was £3,333. But when November 1940 came we said: 'It cannot happen again, but we must try!'

We tried to think of something appropriate for children to subscribe to. I finally suggested a Mobile X-Ray Unit to be called 'The Children's Hour'. On Sunday afternoon, November 10, I made the Appeal, asking for £1,500. After a few days Mr. B. E. Astbury, of the Charity Organisation Society, who organised a shoal of voluntary helpers, wrote: 'I am afraid you will be disappointed this year; donations are not coming in as fast as usual.'

Quickly there followed a more encouraging note, and after that the pace got faster and faster. By the end of December the total was past £15,000!

In the dark days of January 1941 Mac had serious matters to impart. From 1945, the regular Christmas appeals, which raised thousands of pounds, were placed within the category of The Week's Good Cause *(Radio Times 24 January 1941).*

combined with the existing 'For the Children' spots produced by Dearmer.

Previously the Sunday programmes had consisted of monthly special services, which had started as long ago as 1926. The first *Joan and Betty's Bible Stories* was broadcast in 1930. There had been other notable religious programmes concerning the lives of famous Christians, all produced by Dearmer assisted by Lance Sieveking. Now, with the closer ties, more effort was put into making Sunday teatime into an enjoyable family hour. Biographical plays by L. du Garde Peach and adaptations of literature classics swelled the numbers of listeners, and then in December 1941 the BBC launched its most ambitious religious project to date.

In a slightly apprehensive *Radio Times* article, Dr Welch introduced the plays and told a little about the preparation of the series. He had approached Dorothy L. Sayers, famous for her detective stories, asking her if she would write a series of plays about the life of Christ. She had already written a Nativity play called *He That Should Come*, in 1938, and she agreed to the project as long as she could introduce Christ as a full character and not the bland, symbolic figure he was usually portrayed to be. She also wanted to update the language. Welch, treading carefully, made an agreement with the Lord Chamberlain, although this was not strictly necessary, and on Miss Sayers' insistence asked Val Gielgud to produce the series. Robert Speaight was chosen to play Christ. On the Forces network, *The Brains Trust* clashed with the time of the Sunday Children's Hour and its time was changed.

The greatest fear of everyone concerned was the public's attitude towards the plays, which the Lord's Day Observance Society had already condemned as 'bordering on blasphemous' – and this without even reading a word of the script! Miss Sayers had said that she wished to get away from the 'genteel piety and the stained-glass manner', and this attitude caused uproar in the Press of the day – so much that she threatened to bring a libel action against one newspaper. The final decision to broadcast lay in the hands of the General Religious Advisory Committee, who gave their go-ahead to the initial programme; the public's response proved their decision to be correct. All this turmoil was over the series called *The Man Born to be King*. It was probably the first dramatisation of the life of Christ to be broadcast in any country. Although hailed as a great breakthrough, having a high-quality cast, excellent direction, and enjoying enduring popularity, the cycle of plays was never again broadcast in full.

The Schools Repertory Company moved to Bristol in February 1940, and schools broadcasts continued throughout the war, providing a useful unifying teaching aid, especially to those evacuee children being taught in houses and small groups. Under the heading *Let the Children Listen*, a new series of daytime programmes had begun in January. These were 'a cross between Children's Hour and schools broadcasts'. They centred on a Mr Cobbett and his adventures. The first was *Mr Cobbett and the Indians*.

As well as these adventure talks, articles in *Radio Times* encouraged further work on the topics with which the radio shows had dealt. They

ICE TWOPENCE

PROGRAMMES FOR
February 9 — 15

RADIO TIMES

JOURNAL OF THE BRITISH BROADCASTING CORPORATION

(INCORPORATING WORLD-RADIO)

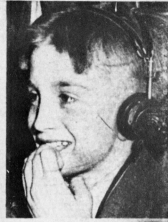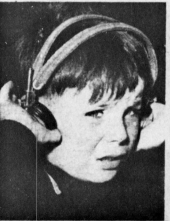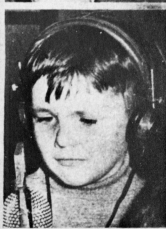

CHILDREN
CALLING
HOME'

Laughter and tears as British children evacuated to America hear the voices of their parents by radio from Britain. The third programme in which children in Canada and America exchange greetings with their parents in this country will be broadcast on Sunday afternoon ● An article by Enid Maxwell on her work in connection with these programmes, the first of an interesting new weekly series of articles entitled '1941 with the BBC', will be found on page 3.

Children Calling Home *from evacuees in Canada and USA* . . . (Radio Times *7 February 1941*).

provided a subtle introduction to arithmetic, history, geography, writing and drawing. Pamphlets were issued in conjunction with the series and Cobbett Clubs grew up, showing their influence and popularity.

Programmes not organised by the Children's Hour section but which proved popular with children and adults alike were those which enabled children to speak to relatives abroad or, like *Children Calling Home*, gave children forced to live in Canada and USA the opportunity to speak to their families in Britain.

Many of the programmes on the Children's Hour were openly patriotic. There were items on how children could be useful during the hostilities by saving, salvaging and harvesting. There were practical lessons on safety, and even John Snagge gave instructions in the use of gas masks. The aim was never to glorify war, but the part being played by the men and women of the Services was never forgotten. On Sunday 13 October 1940 Princess Elizabeth made her first broadcast in Children's Hour, with Princess Margaret joining her in a 'goodnight' at the end.

Olive Shapley, formerly organiser in Manchester, began working in the BBC's New York office, and sent a fortnightly *Letter from America* which started in 1942. One such programme included a message from Mrs Eleanor Roosevelt, and another had a contribution from Sub-Lieutenant W. E. Davis (David), who had enlisted in the Royal Naval Volunteer Reserve. In the series *The House of Westminster* Megan Lloyd George spoke to her young British audience, now learning to live with the realities of war. But that audience had at least one hour each day when it could escape into another world with *The Prisoner of Zenda* and *Little Lord Fauntleroy*, or could be entertained by the adventures of Arthur Ransome's Big Six. For the very young there were Martin Armstrong's *Said the Cat to the Dog* and *Bitty and Bears* by Elizabeth Gorrell.

In 1943 children were saddened by the death of Romany, but David Seth-Smith, L. Hugh Newman, Stephen King-Hall and other regulars continued to broadcast. Evacuee children were able to learn more of their new country surroundings from A. G. Street, Ralph Wightman and A. W. Ling. Syd Walker (famous with adult audiences for his 'What would you do, chums?') told stories on the Hour; Reginald Gamble encouraged the young to take an interest in beekeeping; Robb Wilton was heard as Mr Muddlecombe; Wilfred Pickles became a regular contributor from the North; and Gladys Cooper took the title role in a play about the explorer Mary Kingsley written by E. Arnot Robertson.

The very young were told stories of Tammy Troot, Badger and Mole (from *The Wind in the Willows*), Matilda Mouse and Sam Pig. Sam first appeared in Alison Uttley's book *Tales of Four Pigs and Brock the Badger*. You may recall Sam as the youngest of the four who just 'got in everybody's way, for he was young and simple'. In the pockets of his patched trousers he kept a frog, pieces of honeycomb, a bee or two, snail shells and pebbles, as well as Jemima the fieldmouse and her children.

60

Uncle Mac told stories of Mary Plain and the Mostly Mary tales about the bears that lived in a pit in Berne, Switzerland. He was forced to have several breaks during this period because of ill-health, and in one article he was reported to be convalescing after his forty-fourth operation. He was, however, able to host a series of outside broadcasts devoted to Our Great Railway Systems and help run *Regional Round*, a quiz involving all the regions, which continued for many years after the war. *Worzel Gummidge*, created by Barbara Euphan Todd, made a return in 1945 after delighting children ten years before. Even Sandy Macpherson, who almost single-handed played the BBC through the first few weeks of the war, was conscripted for Children's Hour duty.

When Victory Day came, it was reflected in the five o'clock programmes. There was *Tammy Troot's Victory Day* by Lavinia Derwent, *Praise and Thanksgiving Music* by Helen Henschel, and *Matilda Mouse's Victory Story* by Dora Broome. For Sunday, L. du Garde Peach (who else?) wrote a special victory play called *England Expects*, which was produced by Mac with music by the BBC Symphony Orchestra conducted by Sir Adrian Boult. The children's programmes remained on what had been the spot on the dial provided for home listeners, whereas that of the Forces network became the Light Programme.

In the spring of 1944 the adventures of Norman and Henry Bones, boy detectives, were heard for the first time. They were written by schoolmaster Anthony C. Wilson and produced by Josephine Plummer. Charles Hawtrey played the part of Norman, and after the first two episodes the role of Henry, his cousin, was taken by Patricia Hayes. You may remember the boys lived in a village called Sedgewick in Norfolk. Plots involved jewel thieves, secret panels, spies, dark old houses – the essentials of mystery and adventure for small boys and girls. Wilson had already tested out his stories on the boys at the preparatory school where he taught. The stories of intrigue and excitement remained popular until the passing of the Hour some twenty years later. Request weeks which, like the postal competitions, had been discontinued during the war, were revived in the autumn of 1945. John Buchan's *Salute to Adventure* series began in 1946, and later in that year 'Taffrail' (Captain Taprell Dorling), a writer of sea stories, started the first of several serialised stories of adventure on the high seas. These included *Mid-Atlantic SOS* and *The Chase and Sinking of the Bismarck*.

The programmes were produced by David Davis, who was himself shipwrecked on the way to Anzio and ended up in hospital. Biggles adventures became favourites, with Jack Watson as Major James Bigglesworth. The adaptations of Captain W. E. Johns' famous books were by Bertha Lonsdale. Biggles and his chums Ginger, Algy and Bert were to have their adventures revived on television, but Clara Chuff had to be content with national fame on radio.

Clara Chuff, engine number 30093, was the creation of Harry Harrison, who was inspired to write the stories by a train he saw on the quay at Poole.

Just William was broadcast as a weekly series on the Light Programme, but had a large following among children. Here William, played by John Clark, is in the thick of another family squabble.

Young listeners were treated to these stories in the first fifteen minutes of the Hour – the spot traditionally reserved for the very young – and treated also to the distinctive voice of Johnny Morris, who took many parts in the tales.

In 1946 the Hour, almost always a misnomer, was increased to fifty-five minutes every day, including Sundays. The weather report at 5.55 pm followed the children's programmes, and Gillie Potter remarked at the time when speaking 'to England': 'The weather forecast . . . carried by courtesy of the Children's Hour!'

Another show which was to have great impact in the late forties and early fifties on radio, and later to give rise to numerous television series, was *Just William*. Although not part of Children's Hour, these shows held a massive family audience glued to their receivers at 8 pm every Tuesday. The programmes were repeated on Sunday afternoon at 2.30 pm, but because many young listeners complained they were at Sunday School and missed them, the BBC obligingly changed the time to three o'clock.

The stories were adapted by Alick Hayes from Richmal Crompton's famous books, and it was he who discovered John Clark, who became the first radio William, when he heard him talking on a bus! The programmes began in October 1945 with three adaptations on successive weeks, and their popularity was immediate. The producers rightly felt they had bridged the gap between their young and older audiences and had devised the 'perfect family entertainment'. After this first success they realised that to enable a long run to be broadcast, completely new stories would have to be introduced every week, and with the author's permission they did just that.

In 1947 Rex Diamond, who became one of the co-writers, wrote: 'The reaction to *Just William* by listeners was a pleasant revelation, and proved that here, maybe, was a turning point in light entertainment . . . each week a new plot, situations, and an effective pay-off has to be found.' One of the very first situation comedies was in for a long run. Members of that original cast included Jacqueline Boyer as Violet Elizabeth, Gordon McLeod as William's father, and Charles Hawtrey as bad boy Hubert Lane. In subsequent series, David Spenser took the part of William, Anthea Askey that of Violet Elizabeth, Bruce Belfrage became Mr Brown, and Enid Trevor his wife.

The William programmes became so popular that Mac complained of the possibility of losing some of his Children's Hour audience. Norman Collins dismissed the complaint, perhaps thinking that competition could only improve Children's Hour standards.

A series of holiday programmes was tried in 1949 for children out of school. Lionel Gamlin was the host of the daily shows, which began at noon in the Light Programme. They consisted of several different items, with much more emphasis placed on entertainment than in the tea-time programmes. They often had stars to entertain including Harry Hemsley, Gracie Fields, Percy Edwards and Elton Hayes. They had Biggles adventures, tours around film studios, and altogether a more lighthearted approach than Children's Hour.

In the 1950s the Hour maintained its large audience until television reception began to spread throughout Britain. As late as 1958 the section still received 31,000 letters in the request week. A survey carried out in 1942 had shown that Children's Hour was the third most popular activity for children, after playing outdoors and going to the cinema. Now with television, and especially with the advent of a second channel in 1955, sound radio slipped further down the list.

In 1957 David Davis circulated a long and detailed memorandum to his staff reiterating the aims, approach and plans for Children's Hour. In it he stressed that the staff of the section had built up an enormous experience in entertaining children and a knowledge of what was and what was not accepted by them. He dealt with taboos, how to achieve thrilling tension and suspense without terrifying an audience, how to make talks, poetry and music interesting, and specified numerous details of approach and planning. He was fighting to preserve the Hour with an analysis of where it should go from there.

New programmes had been devised to move with the times. There was *Children's Newsreel* from the North Region, *Saturday Excursion* from London, and the sports programme *Play Up* from the Midlands. Children's Hour had been regularly transmitted for two years by the Overseas Service, and certainly all was not yet lost to television. But whether the Hour would survive, Davis thought, lay in the hands of parents. He wrote: 'Those who believe in, and want their children to enjoy, the things that sound alone can give: the freeing and setting to work of the child's imagination; active, as opposed to passive participation; such parents will continue to make up our audience, and they are not a negligible quantity . . . Sound has good cards to play, and it is the aim and intention of this department to play them.' R. D'A. Marriott, Assistant Director of Sound Broadcasting, however, admitted he was 'at a loss ' as to the future of the Hour.

A children's broadsheet was started in 1955 and lasted for five years. Much discussion was given over to precisely which age group the programmes should now be aimed at, and new names were thought of for the Hour (these included *Home from School*, *Junior Time* and *Home for the Holidays*). The Children's Hour department was renamed Children's Programmes department.

By 1960 there were more adults than children listening to Children's Hour, and it was now to be called *Home at Five* – an hour for the family. To make the shows streamlined, station identification was omitted and continuity was tightened up, with a London announcer acting as MC for the regional offerings.

Programmes for the younger generation on the Light Programme attracted teenagers, while the Hour continued to produce excellent drama from the pens of Angus McVicar, Geoffrey Morgan and Noel Streatfeild, and maintained old favourites like *Nature Parliament* and *Toytown*; but even these were now recorded on discs, produced by Claire Chovil and Josephine Plummer.

There was still 'good' music in *Music Room*, commendable adaptations of the classics, Laurence Olivier reading Bible stories on Sundays, and Patrick Moore discussing the more technical aspects of the heavens in *Star Talk*. The story was still an important ingredient, with such great exponents as David Davis and Johnny Morris practising the art. Morris went on to tell stories on television as the Hot Chestnut Man before his animal and travel programmes.

The Children's Hour was eventually called *For the Young*, and then on 27 March 1964, after a recording of a story read by David called 'The Selfish Giant', it was all over. This microcosm of broadcasting, one of the true radio art forms, the department that had been the pioneer in many fields, was gone. It had achieved many broadcasting 'firsts', including the first play written for radio (by Arthur Burrows) and the first orchestral piece broadcast by a BBC ensemble (Roger Quilter's 'Children's Overture'); while the first stories told on radio were for children.

Back in 1925, on Boxing Day, Jack Payne and his band had played in Children's Hour. That was their first broadcast and their way into radio. Although the famous woodland song of the nightingale had first been transmitted in May 1924, the Children's Hour was the first to present zoo noises, in November of that year. It was one of the first sections to undergo audience research – in 'searchlight enquiries' carried out in January 1938.

Yet another 'first' had been achieved when programmes were recorded for overseas in 1932. These included a Children's Hour broadcast of *Robin Hood and the Sorrowful Knight*. Quizzes, too, were originally allowed only on the shows for children, as they were somewhat frowned upon as being too inconsequential for adult listening.

The diversity of material in the Hour was vast, the quality outstanding, and the atmosphere near perfect for Reith's original aim of subliminal cultural education. So why, then, did it end in 1964? Was it a recurring quirk of the BBC to kill off its successes? Had children changed so much that the format was out of date? Was the Hour interfering with arrangements for other programmes?

John Snagge and Michael Barsley in their book *Those Vintage Years of Radio* come to the conclusion that it could have been all of these. Whatever the Corporation's reasons for its curtailment, the most obvious one was that

Top of the Form *on an international scale: London* v. *Scandinavia in 1951. The questionmaster on this occasion was Wynford Vaughan-Thomas.*

listeners were becoming viewers by the thousand. The numbers listening to children's radio were greatly diminished, but some would say still sufficient for the BBC to provide an alternative to the box. Norman Shelley said that the decision to close that section of broadcasting was 'nothing but assassination'.

Certain programmes for children did remain, though these were not provided by the Children's Hour team. *Top of the Form*, which had begun in 1948, was devised and produced by Joan Clarke. She had joined the BBC in 1935 as a secretary, and became a producer in variety and a scriptwriter as well as an interviewer on *In Town Tonight* and a *Radio Newsreel* producer. The quiz between schools has had many questionmasters, including Lionel Gamlin, Robert MacDermot, John Ellison, Tim Gudgin, Geoffrey Wheeler and Paddy Feeney, with Joan Clarke acting as scorer for many years. International games were started as early as 1950, and the competition became equally popular on television. The radio version continues to provide competition between Britain's schoolchildren.

Children's Favourites has been a regular early morning weekend record show since January 1954. It was Pat Osborne who, while sorting out requests for a *Housewives' Choice* programme in the 1940s, noticed that a great many were from children, and decided to keep these back for a special programme on Saturday when more children would be at home. There were protests that the children already had a daily programme, and the idea was then dropped.

Some years later – in 1953 – when Donald Peers was compère of *Housewives' Choice* during the Christmas period, he suggested that a Christmas morning edition for children might be a good idea, and announced it over the air. The resultant mail was the biggest postbag ever received. Because many of the children inevitably had to be disappointed that their requests could not be played, it was decided to repeat the children's show on the following Saturdays, and this time there were no complaints.

The show was called *Children's Choice*, but in January the name was changed to *Children's Favourites*, and Mac returned from retirement to compère the first editions. Other presenters in the earlier years included Rex Palmer, Peter Brough (with Archie Andrews), Max Bygraves and John Ellison. The programmes have always had a wide range of music and comedy, from light classics to nursery rhymes, from old favourites to the latest popular music. Over the last ten years the bias has been towards pop music, with Ed Stewart (Stewpot) and more recently Tony Blackburn playing the 'discs' (Mac only played 'records'). Stewart, with his 'Morning' and 'Byeee' catchphrases and the 'Happy Birthday' and 'Ello darlin'' jingles, proved an excellent successor to the early presenters.

His two famous jingles, incidentally, were taken from an interview he did with a boy in hospital on a 'special'. With the massive coverage of pop music today it is pleasant occasionally to hear that a youngster has found sufficient

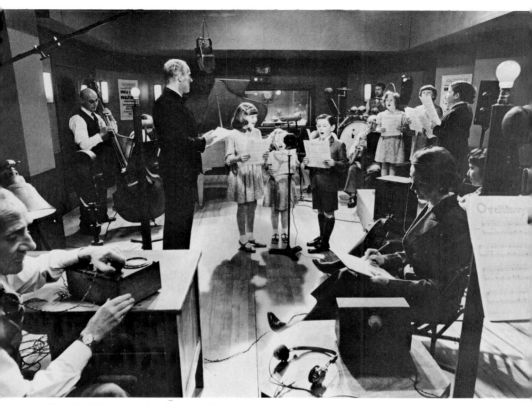

The Ovaltineys, a classic of Radio Luxembourg pre- and post-war, singing enthusiastically in the studio. Other European stations, such as Normandy with its Nursery Corner, *had programmes for children. To have your birthday greetings read on Radio Normandy you had to send two shillings – but it* was *a commercial station!*

enjoyment from an 'oldie' like 'Three Little Fishes' or 'Sparky's Magic Piano' to want to request it again.

It cannot be said that the BBC had a complete monopoly of the entertainment of British children on the radio, for there were European stations broadcasting popular music most of the evening which could be received on British radios. One programme almost achieved the popularity of Children's Hour. It was broadcast from Radio Luxembourg, and was sponsored by the makers of Ovaltine. The firm had set up a club called The League of Ovaltineys and ran the Sunday evening show in conjunction. It was called *The Ovaltiney Concert Party*, and for part of its run was compèred by Harry Hemsley, well-known broadcaster of the day, with his fictitious children Elsie, Johnny, Winnie, and of course Baby Horace.

Listening now to recordings of the children's chorus with its wavering, high-pitched voices evokes memories of cosy rooms, dressing-gowns and perhaps even a warm beverage. This nostalgia has been used to good effect in Wander Foods' more recent advertisements (including TV commercials). One of the singing Ovaltineys was none other than Leslie Crowther, who went on to entertain children and adults alike several years later. The club, which started in 1937, reached a peak membership of over five million, and although it was suspended during the war its popularity did not begin to wane until the fifties. It was finally disbanded in 1957.

6
Were *You* Sitting Comfortably?

It was in 1950 that the BBC first attempted to provide entertainment for those too young to listen with much appreciation to Children's Hour by starting a new trial programme, *Listen With Mother*. It was envisaged that a six-month period would prove whether it was to be a success or failure. With over thirty years under its belt, it eventually qualified as one of the most successful children's programmes of all time.

Three freelance presenters were originally used, each providing one month's programmes. The first was Julia Lang, and it was she who first posed the famous question, 'Are you sitting comfortably?' Daphne Oxenford was the next, and the third month was dealt with by Catherine Edwards. The first story told was called 'Peter the Black Kitten' and Julia Lang soon became known as 'The Pussy Lady'. Daphne Oxenford remembers clearly so many of those early stories and the Monday recording sessions of the week's stories and songs, which were recorded, though the Monday show was always put out live.

Letters immediately began to flow back from that new excited audience, addressed to 'Junior Lamb', 'Daffy Awkward', and 'Dotty Sniff'. The last named was Dorothy Smith, another of those early storytellers. The letters contained paintings, stories, questions such as, 'Please, where do you go when you say goodbye?' and comments such as, 'How clever of my lady to know I was going to Granny today. She came *there* to tell me my story.' When Lorna Pegram joined the programme she was renamed 'Lorna Penguin' by the children.

George Dixon, a senior schools producer with a long and distinguished career in broadcasting, sang songs and read nursery rhymes; a definite policy of repetition stemmed from an intuitive knowledge of young children's patterns of learning and enjoyment. The songs of George Dixon and Eileen Browne, one of the clerical staff, were often unaccompanied and, although the singers were obviously trained, it was hoped that they would sound like 'anybody's uncle singing in the bath'. It was also hoped that the level of enjoyment could easily be matched by the listening child's parents,

Julia Lang – the first presenter of Listen With Mother. *The original idea was brought back from Australia by Mary Somerville, who heard a programme there called* Kindergarten of the Air.

and would perhaps encourage them to sing and tell stories to their children afterwards. There cannot have been many of my generation who did not march up and down the hill with 'The Grand Old Duke of York' in the company of George Dixon.

Miss Oxenford pays great tribute to the producer and guiding light of the programme for many years, Jean Sutcliffe. It was she who planned the broadcasts, wrote some of the scripts and studied the effect that each item

Daphne Oxenford – another presenter of Listen With Mother. *I remember how clever I thought I was, aged four, because I could imitate the programme's beginning: 'When the music stops, Daphne Oxenford will be here to speak to you.'*

might have on the young audience. Care was taken in preparation, but unforeseen problems sometimes occurred.

In the early days parents wrote to ask if the 'klink-klonk' of horses' hooves could be removed from the end of *Humpty Dumpty* as their children thought they were going to gallop out of the radio. After a short story by Julia Lang where a boy went 'splish, splash, splosh' through puddles, the producer was asked if they could stress that before he did it he put on his wellingtons!

Jean Sutcliffe was meticulous with her facts: when a story came in about a child going to visit its granny in Birmingham, bus timetables were consulted and checked for accuracy lest any child had taken the same trip and might write in to point out mistakes.

The storytellers wrote several of their own tales, and Daphne Oxenford remembers reading one sent in by a young child; it was about a train called 'Chak-a-dee-der' and needed just a little tidying up before it was broadcast. Some of the stories and characters became great favourites. Dorothy Smith's readings of the My Naughty Little Sister stories written by the late Dorothy Edwards are still remembered with affection.

It was schools broadcasting which had the responsibility for providing the fifteen minutes at 1.45 pm each day. Although children were never deliberately taught, they were able to pick up ideas such as counting from rhymes such as 'One, Two, Three, Four, Five – Once I Caught a Fish Alive', and to listen to good quality music, a few bars of which often opened the programme after, of course, the 'bong-be-bong' of its evocative opening theme.

The claim of some critics that the programme was very middle class and cosy is refuted by Miss Oxenford, who feels that all the presenters considered themselves ordinary adults entertaining ordinary children, and a three-year-old is a three-year-old whatever his or her background. She does remember, however, that Jean Sutcliffe was once told by a Harley

The familiar phrases even reached the cartoon strips. Here are two examples of the 'Clive' cartoon by Angus McGill.

Street doctor that he recommended listening to *Listen With Mother* as speech therapy for some of his patients, as in it they would hear clear, precise, impersonal speech.

It was not only children and their parents who listened, but seamen on board ship were also regular listeners, as were the occupants of Buckingham Palace. One day when Daphne Oxenford was shopping, a lady approached her saying that her young child insisted that Miss Oxenford told her stories on the wireless. The child had realised this just from hearing Miss Oxenford in the shop, but her disbelieving parent and Miss Oxenford were amazed that this could be true, as the child and her mother had only just returned from living as a 'Service' family in Germany.

The audience numbers diminished over the years with the advent of *Watch With Mother* and other television alternatives, and *Listen With Mother* latterly commanded only 0.7 per cent of the two- to five-year-olds, whereas *Play School* had 70 per cent of this age range. There were changes in transmission times which may have reduced the audience even more. New presenters such as Tony Aitken tried to to maintain a gentle traditional simplicity while endeavouring to keep the programme alive; however, despite great public outcry the programme finally ended in 1982.

7

Schools Broadcasting

One could not write commentary on the history of broadcasting for children without mention of schools broadcasting – although one may regard it rather like the school timetable, as useful and necessary, but not look back on it with the same fondness as playtime and old school friends. Nevertheless, memories of singing songs around the classroom speaker and 'music and movement' do stand out as some of the more exciting moments in the school day.

Even today, when radio and television are no longer novel or magical, the lesson which utilises the TV aid still generates increased enthusiasm and interest. This may well be because the child is transported from the classroom to foreign lands, into factories, or even back in time. It was some time before the early broadcasters to schools recognised this unique potential. It could provide the young listener or viewer with something that no classroom-bound teacher could achieve individually without great expense.

Broadcasting to schools began in 1924. At that time a new policy for education had recently been developed, and it was believed that broadcasting 'could bring great teachers to permeate the elementary school with the standards of the universities'. J. C. Stobart was seconded from the Board of Education to direct the BBC's approach, and many teachers began to raise money to buy sets.

One of the earliest speakers was Sir Walford Davies, whose musical appreciation programmes provided a new period in the schools curriculum. Others finding their feet in the new medium were Geoffrey Shaw, E. Kay Robinson, Professor Lyde and Sir Stanley Leathes.

The programmes did not meet with universal approval. Some teachers disliked the idea of a single organisation – the BBC – planning to influence education and perhaps affect the staffing levels. Would a voice from a box hold the child's attention after the novelty had worn off? Some thought that education could be achieved only by an intimate contact between teacher and pupil. Complaints that Sir Walford's programmes were taken at too

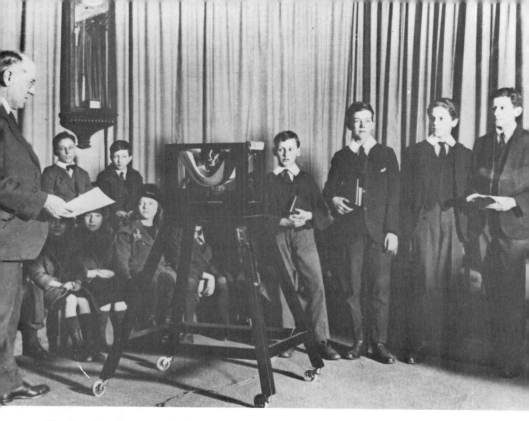

The first broadcast to schools: Sir Walford Davies with choirboys of the Temple Church, April 1924. A pioneer of music broadcasting, especially to schools, Davies once quoted Matthew Arnold to illustrate the microphone technique he used: 'Have something to say and say it as simply as you can.'

quick a pace, and that many words and phrases used were not understood by the bulk of children, led eventually to his having a 'watchdog' listening to him in a classroom and reporting back. Feedback was beginning. It was said that certain presenters tended to talk down to children. Extensive trials were carried out in the schools of Kent for over a year, and as a result a marked change came over the format and content of transmissions.

A philosophy developed to provide a window on the world, to quote *Panorama*'s phrase, and to minimise the 'teacher in the box' impression. Dramatised histories became very popular, as did personal experience, whether it be Alan Sullivan talking about his visits to Eskimos or Ernest Haddon telling of his contact with pygmies. Eric Parker went on walks and spoke about flowers and animals. Sound-pictures of science, work and history were presented. The lesson learned from Children's Hour of 'dissolving the studio walls' began to work. It was realised that a child must first enjoy a cultural activity in order to appreciate it, and so the material presented should be pitched at exactly the right level.

Feedback from teachers was an essential part of the programme planning, and the programme sub-committees started to play an active part in advising the Central Council for Schools Broadcasting (formed in 1929 under the chairmanship of the Rt Hon. H. A. L. Fisher). Mary Somerville OBE was Director of Schools Broadcasting from 1929 until 1947, and in that time the variety of programmes available to teachers increased perhaps beyond even her early expectations. Although, as expressed in the *BBC Handbook* for 1931, there were reservations about the scope that sound broadcasting could offer for the teaching of mathematics and science, many doubts have since been shown to be ill-conceived. Any gaps in radio education were filled when television took up its educative role.

In July 1937 Sir John Reith opened the Welsh Region station, and schools broadcasts, leaflets and books from the BBC had to be available in two languages. In that same year the London County Council issued a report on broadcast lessons in London elementary schools in which they stated that they should be 'unique, fascinating, dramatic, coloured and new, coming as it were from a world which teachers and pupils without their help cannot enter. The broadcaster should not be concerned primarily with teaching the facts, rather he should use all the resources at his disposal in order to provide stimulating educational experiences for his listeners.' By 1938 the BBC was

At the receiving end: Elstow School, September 1926.

offering programmes in a wide range of subjects, including music, history, geography, science, English and foreign languages, but with the outbreak of war the service was more irregularly used. Yet the number of schools equipped with radios still increased. Special priority was given to broadcasts about America in geography and current affairs programmes.

By the end of the war the BBC was transmitting thirty-nine programmes a week and introduced talks to sixth forms on problems of the day; Ann Driver was inspiring young dancers with her *Music and Movement*; and over 12,000 schools were equipped with radios. Through the facilities of the Transcription Unit, schools programmes began to be sent to all parts of the world. By 1950 regular programmes were being sent to most parts of the

Schools broadcasting carried on, with its curriculum unimpaired. Rhoda Power developed, to great effect, dramatisation of historic events – and earned this backhanded compliment from a young listener. 'Dear Rhoda Power, I love this history. When I grow up, I am going to be a history teacher like you, for by that time I shall have reached the years of transgression.' (Radio Times *12 April 1940*).

CHOOL BROADCASTING IN WARTIME SUMMER TERM April 15 to June 2

MONDAYS	TUESDAYS	WEDNESDAYS	THURSDAYS	FRIDAYS	
Singing Together by Herbert Wiseman Ages 9-11	Physical Training * (for use in halls) by Edith Dowling Ages 9-12	Music and Movement * by Ann Driver Ages 7-9	Music for Every Day * The Adventure of Music by Ronald Biggs Ages 9-15	Music and Movement * by Ann Driver Ages 5-7	11.0
Interval Music	Interval Music	Current Affairs	Interval Music	Senior English * Rhyme and Reason by A G Strong Ages 13-15	11.2 11.2
World History * Servants of the World; Modern Times Planned by Rhoda Power Ages 9-12	Junior English * Games with Words Arranged by Douglas Allan Ages 9-12	Ages 13 and over	English for Under-Nines * Ten-Minute Tales by Rhoda Power Ages 7-9 Interval Music	Interval Music	11.
Senior English * Book Talks by S. P. B. Mais Ages 11-15	Talks for Fifth Forms * Science and the Community Planned by J. Lauwerys (Beginning May 7) Ages 15 and over	For Home Listening * Mr. Cobbett in North Africa Written by E. Arnot Robertson Ages 7-12	Senior Geography * The Far East Planned by G. R. Taylor Ages 11-15	Talks for Sixth Forms * (Beginning May 3) Ages 16 and over	11. 1.
The Practice and Science of Gardening * The Garden in Wartime by B. A. Keen and C. F. Lawrence Ages 11-15	For Rural Schools * The Food of Britain by John R. Allan Ages 9-15	Music Making * Sir Walford Davies Ages 9-15	Nature Study * Round the Countryside Ages 9-12	Travel Talks * Peoples of the Empire Planned by E. G. R. Taylor Ages 9-12	2
Interval Music		Interval Music	Interval Music	Interval Music	2
Preparatory Concert Broadcasts * Musical Scenes and Stories Planned by John Horton Ages 9-15	For Under-Sevens * Let's Join In with Ann Driver and Jean Sutcliffe Senior English * Good Writing	Biology * Our Daily Life by A. D. Peacock and R. C. Garry Ages 11-15 Interval Music	Physical Training * (for use in class-rooms) by Edith Dowling Ages 9-12 Interval Music	If You Were French Ages 11-15	2 2
Interval Music English for Under-Nines * Action Stories and Plays Planned by Jean Sutcliffe Ages 7-9		Junior English * Plays, Stories and Poems Planned by Jean Sutcliffe Ages 9-12	British History * Britain Finds Herself Ages 11-15	Gwersi Cymraeg * 1 Storiau a Llenyddiaeth Ages 9-12 2 Hanes Cymru Ages 11-15	2

For these series Teachers' Leaflets (1½d. each) are issued. English Schools should apply to : The British Broadcasting Corporation, Scarle Road, Wembley, Middlesex ; tish Schools to : The Secretary, Scottish Council for School Broadcasting, Broadcasting House, Queen Margaret Drive, Glasgow, W.1 ; Welsh Schools to : The Secretary, Welsh Committee, C.C.S.B., 39, Park Place, Cardiff.

Mary Somerville, who played a major part in the development of schools broadcasting.

Spanish-speaking countries of Latin America, and many experimental programmes to several English-speaking countries. By then Richmond Postgate was Head of Schools Broadcasting. As a result of the Commonwealth Broadcasting Conference of 1952 a programme exchange scheme between Commonwealth countries was undertaken.

In the same year the BBC carried out an experimental closed-circuit schools television service in six schools in Middlesex. Although a full service was tentatively planned for 1953, the plan was shelved.

1952 – and experimental television reached the classroom of six schools in Middlesex.

Paul Adorian, a radio engineer who had worked extensively with visual aids in the war, tried to interest the BBC in a schools TV service, but apart from the closed-circuit experiment, nothing was achieved at that time. In 1956 he became managing director of Associated Rediffusion, and laid plans for schools broadcasts which were tried the same year.

Although teachers remained sceptical and suspicious of the company's motives, Adorian continued with his experiment, and an Education Advisory Committtee was set up in 1957. It was chaired by Sir John Wolfenden. On 13 May the first programme transmitted as the beginning of a regular schools broadcasting service was called *Looking and Seeing*, and was designed for fourteen- and fifteen-year-olds. The programme could be seen only in the London and Midland areas and then only by the estimated eighty schools which had sets.

On 24 September 1957, at the request of the Schools Broadcasting Council and after consultation with the Ministry of Education, the BBC began a limited nationwide schools TV service. To assist with timetable planning, both the BBC and the Independent Television Authority began to repeat each programme at different times in the same week, a system which continued for many years, though the use of video recorders has now diminished the need for it.

Viewing figures grew so that by 1965 one-third of the country's schools had TV sets. Each channel improved and expanded its range of programmes. To avoid duplication of material, to organise audience research and to discuss other problems, a close liaison grew up between the two rival organisations and a joint committee was formed. It is in schools broadcasting that the BBC and the Independent Broadcasting Authority (as the ITA became in 1972) still enjoy the closest contact. In 1970 both bodies agreed to relax recording copyright restrictions to enable schools to record programmes for future use within one year. Today over 80 per cent of all schools use the services provided by these two organisations.

In 1964 pre-school education took a giant leap forward with the creation, by Joy Whitby (a one-time producer of *Listen With Mother*), of *Play School*. It reflected a hardcore approach: 'in *Play School* a cat is a cat and not a pussy' – a throwback perhaps to the attitude on *Listen With Mother*. The programmes have remained original, witty and absorbing to young viewers for many years. It was one of the first programmes for the very young where a definite mental effort was required from the viewers. When *Play School* and *Andy Pandy* were transmitted at similar times in Australia by ABC, an interesting phenomenon was observed. Interest in *Andy Pandy* diminished somewhat but was maintained in *Play School*, and although parents wanted their children to like the cuddlesome puppets, it was to the thought-provoking format of *Play School* that they paid most attention.

Another development in the education of the very young came in 1971 with the introduction to British screens of the controversial American programme *Sesame Street*. It had been first broadcast in the USA in 1969, and was produced by the non-profit-making Children's TV Workshop. The shows were produced by Joan Ganz, a person dedicated to an improvement in television for children. Jim Henson invented the puppets and outrageous creatures, and continued in the same field to produce the Muppets; Kermit the Frog was originally invented for the *Sesame Street* shows.

Their style was fast-moving, their language often contained Americanisms, and they used a 'hard-sell' approach to education which until then had been seen only in advertisements. The show was originally turned down by Monica Sims for the BBC, but proved to be very successful when shown on ITV. Similar programmes have followed, but none has matched the lavish sets and ebullience of *Sesame Street*.

8
Now You See It . . .

In April 1925 John Logie Baird – son of a Scottish minister, graduate of Glasgow Technical College and inventor of the 'medicated foot sock', a patent type of soap and other miscellaneous items – demonstrated his latest idea. On 27 January 1926 he was invited to demonstrate it to forty members of the Royal Institution.

As early as 1817 J. J. Berzelius, the Swedish scientist, had discovered the means of transmitting tonal shades over distances, and in 1839 Edmund Becquerel discovered the electrochemical effects of light. An accidental discovery – by a telegraph operator called May – that selenium was photosensitive led to new interest in the subject of 'seeing by electricity'. It was Paul Nipkow who first had the idea of the spirally perforated spinning scanner which Baird developed and demonstrated some forty years later in that small room in Frith Street, Soho, calling it his 'televisor'.

The cathode ray tube had been invented in 1897 and had been used to display pictures by Boris Rosing in Russia and Dieckmann in Germany. W. Campbell Swinton suggested using a deflected beam of electrons as the scanning device, and this proposal was acted upon several years later by EMI, a company formed from the Gramophone Company and other organisations. While Baird began perfecting his mechanical system – in which no cathode ray tube was incorporated – EMI, with greater financial backing, developed the 'iconoscope' invented by Vladimir Zworykin for RCA, an associate company in the USA.

In 1929 the BBC began cautious experiments using the relatively poor-definition Baird system with an inaugural service on 30 September. The first simultaneous sight-and-sound transmission was in March 1930, when Gracie Fields performed the historic opening ceremony. The Derby was televised the following year with one solitary camera provided by Baird. Impressed, the BBC commissioned a complete transmitter from Baird's company and equipped a studio at Portland Place. Higher definition pictures of 120 lines had now been developed, and a committee under Lord Selsdon was appointed in 1934 to review the developments and consider the relative merits of the systems then available. It recommended that the BBC should be allowed to develop a public television service, but that the Baird and EMI-Marconi systems should be used alternately and provide pictures of 240-line definition.

Alexandra Palace was chosen as the new home of the BBC television studios, and Gerald Cox became the first Director of Television. He and the staff he appointed were then still learning how television worked, but with enthusiasm began to organise the 'Ally Pally', as it was to be christened by Gracie Fields. The world's first regular television service began from Alexandra Palace at 3.30 pm on Monday 2 November 1936 and, because of the typically British compromise of the Selsdon Committee, it had to cope with the peculiarities of a dual system.

For the first few weeks two one-hour programmes were produced, one in the afternoon and one in the evening, organised by Cecil Madden and his studio manager Peter Bax. Regulars in front of the cameras were Leslie Mitchell (the first male announcer), Jasmine Bligh and Elizabeth Cowell. The range of the service was officially a forty-mile radius from Muswell Hill, although reports of reception far outside this area were common. Baird housed all his television equipment in the Crystal Palace – which burnt down in November and all he had was lost. With this setback and the growing awareness that the mechanical system had severe limitations Baird finally lost his battle with EMI-Marconi, who had meantime developed a 405-line picture. In 1937 the Baird system was finally dropped.

Alexandra Palace was chosen as the site of the BBC's first station because of its hilltop situation some 300 feet above sea level. It provided sufficient space for two studios, about 5000 square feet on the upper floor, with the ground floor housing the transmitters. Over several years new offices and other buildings were added, but only a portion of the original building was used. Only the two studios were built and the restrictions caused by the limited space were evident in the programme schedules, with only a few hours' broadcasting in any one day and closedowns between afternoon and evening transmissions to allow time for studio arrangements and rehearsals.

Scenery movements were often halted for five minutes while an announcement was made in one corner of Studio B, only to continue when Studio A was back on the air. Teatime children's programmes were difficult in these conditions, but attempts were made to interest children with programmes such as *The Zoo Today*, presented by David Seth-Smith. Cecil Madden, a friend of Walt Disney, introduced Mickey Mouse cartoons to television, and it was one of these which ended the television service at noon on Friday, 1 September 1939. Without warning, British television closed down, and was to remain closed for nearly seven years. At the time of its closedown, the service still had only 25,000 viewers.

'The Television March' by Eric Coates welcomed viewers back to the BBC's television service on the afternoon of 7 June 1946, with Jasmine Bligh speaking the opening words. Maurice Gorham was now Head of Television, and many of the old staff returned. After the opening ceremony what should appear but that Mickey Mouse cartoon, *Mickey's Gala Premiere*, which had served to close the pre-war service.

Incidentally, the Disney studios were then allowing cartoons to be screened, but their full-length features were never to appear on the small screen. Some film companies did not allow screening of any of their material, such was the threat they considered television posed to cinemas. It was predicted that the popularity of TV would herald the demise not only of the cinema but also of sportsgoing, the theatre, family musicmaking, the pursuit of hobbies and the reading of books. Probably all these *have* been affected to different degrees.

In the 1950s it was thought that after the 'honeymoon' (as Norman Collins, BBC Controller of Television, called the first few months of viewing), the viewers would sensibly discriminate between what they did and did not want to see by switching off. That was at a time when there were several hours of blank screens every day, and when on or off was the only choice. The advantages and disadvantages of television have been argued about even more than when radio first offered the public a new way of spending leisure time. Without doubt the advent of TV was to change social habits dramatically. By the mid-sixties it was known that children between the ages of twelve and fourteen, by far the most ardent viewers, averaged about sixteen hours of viewing each week. About one child in ten was watching an incredible thirty hours per week.

Children's broadcasts were initially restricted to Sunday, and to one hour. On 21 May 1950 Mrs Attlee, the Prime Minister's wife, was televised opening Studio D at Lime Grove, Shepherds Bush. This was one of five large film studios that the BBC was converting to house a new television centre (the lease on Alexandra Palace was due to expire in 1956). Studio D was to be concerned primarily with the production of children's programmes. Almost immediately the number of sessions for children was increased, and weekly shows on Wednesdays and Fridays were added to the Sunday hour. Soon the service was daily.

The priority the BBC was giving to children's programmes was probably for two reasons: first, because of the educational tradition of the BBC and the great success of its radio service; and second, because of the commercial realisation that there would be increased incentive for parents to buy sets if they thought their children could benefit from such a purchase. The emphasis in programme planning was always on 'wholesome' entertainment. After the children's programmes there was an hour closedown, which enabled parents to switch the children off the television as well as vice versa. This 'toddlers' truce' served as a useful gap to persuade youngsters to do homework or to be packed off to bed.

Seven producers were appointed in 1950/1 to work exclusively on children's programmes, and Richmond Postgate, who had been in charge of schools broadcasting, became their co-ordinator. The most experienced

The mast of Alexandra Palace, famous symbol of BBC TV. The Children's Newsreel used the mast with radiating 'sound waves' in its title.

producer at that time was Peter Thompson, who had helped to build up the Sunday schedule for children. He had worked at Alexandra Palace as a talks producer. Joy Harington had produced some plays for the BBC before her appointment on the children's staff, and was brought in to handle plays for younger viewers. Other members of this pioneer team were Dorothea Brooking, a writer and studio manager for BBC radio who had been trained at the Old Vic; Naomi Capon, who had worked in America teaching drama at Yale University and had acted on American radio; and Pamela Brown, who had previously written for children's radio and also acted in some of her own plays, notably as Sandra in *The Swish of the Curtain*, a radio serial.

Rex Tucker, a writer of children's books, who had worked on Children's Hour back in 1939, became another new children's TV producer, as did Michael Westmore, a law graduate who developed a love of puppets and model theatres and who was to produce the very successful *Whirligig* programmes. Denis Monger had been filing clerk, sound effects boy and producer on radio, and then joined the children's TV unit at about this time.

A special *Children's Newsreel* was launched in 1951 edited by Don Smith, who had worked on the Television Newsreel Unit. Mary Malcolm and Stephen Grenfell became the first commentators for the weekly fifteen-minute programme. The opening title sequence of 'transmission waves' radiating from the mast of Alexandra Palace is one of the indelible memories of the early Lime Grove programmes.

A regular face in front of the camera for three years in the early fifties was child announcer Jennifer Gay. The daughter of an orchestral conductor and an actress, she began her television career at fourteen. She was probably the world's first regular child announcer, and took part in the first cross-Channel hook-up in 1950.

By 1950 the BBC children's programmes had already created a star in their Sunday shows. Without doubt the biggest name in children's entertainment in the late forties and early fifties was that pioneering puppet Muffin the Mule and his presenter Annette Mills. Miss Mills, sister of the actor to become Sir John Mills, had trained as a pianist but dropped that idea, becoming an acrobatic dancer. She joined a musical comedy company playing in South Africa, and while performing in the show fell and broke her leg. She returned to the piano and wrote songs which eventually came to be sung by Stanley Holloway, Beatrice Lillie, Douglas Byng and Frances Day. Her song 'Boomps-a-Daisy' became a best seller and she began singing on the music halls. When the war came Annette went entertaining the troops until one night, while driving between engagements in the blackout, she hit a lorry. She was seriously injured and was in hospital for three years.

Slowly she started to work again, taking part in radio discussion programmes, and one day she was asked if she would sing songs at the piano for children on television. She decided to enhance the programme by using puppets playing on top of the piano as she sang. She asked Ann Hogarth and Jan Bussell if they could help her with one of the puppets from their store.

Muffin the Mule: given life by Ann Hogarth (above) and a personality by his presenter, Annette Mills. While Miss Mills played on the piano for Muffin, Ann Hogarth stood on the back part of the piano behind a crude partition.

She spotted – forgotten on a shelf – a clown and a wooden mule and chose these to be a double act on the first show. The clown she called Crumpet, but he did not look good on the screen and was shelved. The mule was, of course, named Muffin:

> *Here comes Muffin, Muffin the Mule,*
> *Dear old Muffin, playing the fool,*
> *Here comes Muffin, everybody sing*
> *Here comes Muffin the Mule.*

Muffin had been bought by Ann Hogarth from a travelling showman for fifteen shillings but was never really used until he was spotted by Miss Mills. Muffin acquired several friends, including Louise the Lamb, Peregrine the crusty penguin, and Prudence and Primrose Kitten, who were eventually given their own shows. In 1950 Miss Mills was awarded the British Television Society's medal for the most outstanding contribution to television entertainment. She died in 1955, at the height of her fame.

In 1951 Freda Lingstrom became Head of Children's Television. She had joined the BBC in 1942, working in radio in the Home News Talks department, and later moved to Schools Broadcasting.

It was she who was to create those two early favourites of the very young, *Andy Pandy* and *The Flowerpot Men*. Andy Pandy, Teddy, and Looby Loo the doll were the first to occupy the mid-afternoon spot, aimed at the same age group as *Listen With Mother*, and subtitled 'for the very young'. The fact that the strings on these puppets could be obviously seen did not seem to detract from the pleasure of their antics and songs. Andy and his friends, you will remember, lived in a large linen basket and had just a few minutes' freedom each day before they were whisked back and it was

> *Time to go home, time to go home.*
> *Andy is waving goodbye, goodbye.*

Today Andy rests in a metal deed box in the country home of Freda Lingstrom. Maria Bird was the regular storyteller for *Andy Pandy*, and she also wrote the script and songs for this programme and *The Flowerpot Men*. In both series Audrey Atterbury and Molly Gibson pulled the strings. Bill and Ben, the Flowerpot Men, were made audible by the vocal talents of Peter Hawkins, who invented a language for them which consisted of 'flobadobs' and 'flibadobs', but which was almost understandable. 'Was it Bill or was it Ben?' Only 'Ipple weeb', the flower between the plant pots, and we viewers, knew. The next in the series of what became *Watch With Mother* was *Rag, Tag and Bobtail*. Written by Louise Cochrane, these stories were told by Charles E. Stidwill; 'making the pictures' were Sam and Elizabeth Williams. Another favourite was *The Woodentops*, in which there was 'the biggest spotty dog you ever did see'.

Two new child announcers arrived in 1951. These were Elizabeth Croft and Janette Scott, who achieved achieved stardom in films some years later.

Freda Lingstrom, OBE, when head of BBC Television Children's Programmes.

Andy Pandy, Looby Loo and Teddy. Andy was originally brought to life by Freda Lingstrom and Maria Bird on their kitchen table. For those who saw Andy only in black and white – his suit was blue and white.

They were also joined by new puppet characters including Alison Uttley's creation, Little Grey Rabbit, who had been introduced first on radio, and Timothy Telescope, who starred in a magazine programme on Saturday afternoons hosted by Valerie Hobson. The show consisted mainly of handicraft and hobby demonstrations and stories, as well as adventures of a cowboy called Hank who eventually moved to the show which followed Timothy Telescope on Saturdays. That show was called *Whirligig*. Produced by Michael Westmore, the show was to provide teatime entertainment for children on Saturdays for many years. Hank and his friends Silver King, a goofy horse, Cassy, Freddy Parrot and Mexican Pete the bandit (who always managed to get in a chorus of his theme tune – the

Humphrey Lestocq (H.L.) aided by Mr Turnip, introduced Whirligig *from the BBC's Lime Grove studios. Mr Turnip, especially invented for the programme by Joy Laurey, was a bossy character while H.L. was the simple stooge.*

'Mexican Hat Dance'), Big Chief Dirty Face ('Me Big Chief Dirty Face. Me always in disgrace. Ugh!') and their creator Francis Coudrill joined the *Whirligig* regulars.

These were Mr Turnip, Humphrey Lestocq (H.L.), Geoffrey Robinson, Steve Race and Joy Laurey, who invented Mr Turnip. Lestocq had gained fame as Flying Officer Kite in *HMS Waterlogged*, with his catch phrase 'I rather care for that', and now as H.L. was Turnip's foil and mentor with another catch phrase 'Goody, goody gumdrops'. Steve Race looked after the music, and Geoffrey Robinson performed magic and sometimes showed how the tricks were done!

The voice of Mr Turnip was created by Peter Hawkins, whose voice has been heard so often on television from his 'flowerpot' days, in the Captain Pugwash stories, and up to the Dr Who serials where he was an original Dalek. The script for *Whirligig* was written by Peter Ling, who went on to write countless television serials for children on both BBC and ITV and many adult shows, including *Crossroads*. Caudrill was able to outlive *Whirligig* and begin writing, filming and producing his own short features.

Rolf Harris began his long association with children's television on *Whirligig* in later series produced by Desmond O'Donovan. He introduced Willoughby, the drawing-board which came to life.

> *Whirligig, Whirligig, round and round we go.*
> *Whirligig, Whirligig time to say 'Hello!'*
> *Turnip, Hank and H.L.*
> *Want us all to know*
> *It's welcome to Whirligig.*
> *And on with the show!*

Good quality drama was not lacking after the children's spot had been established in the fifties with *The Florentine Apprentice* starring John Slater, the serialisation of *The Secret Garden*, examples of the plays in 1952. In that year also Joy Harington introduced Billy Bunter to the viewing public, with the first of many series of the famous schoolboy stories by Frank Richards. Bunter was played with compelling enthusiasm by Gerald Campion, and Mr Quelch, the form master of the Remove, was played with just the right amount of irascibility by Kynaston Reeves. It was not surprising that the plays had such a large adult following with such excellent casting and delightful stories.

Bunter was revived in the sixties, with Campion still in the role of the 'Fat Owl' but with Frank Melford playing Quelch and new young actors to play Bunter's regular chums Nugent, Cherry, Wharton and the rest. Campion, writing in *Radio Times* in 1960, decided that producing the shows left its mark on the various producers who had attempted it. Shaun Sutton, who produced six episodes, used to cry 'Yarooh' at Campion whenever they met in the BBC corridors. Other cries of 'Beast!', 'I say, you fellows' and 'Go and eat coke' echoed round the walls before they parted. David Hemmings,

Billy Bunter (played by Gerald Campion) confronts his form master, Mr Quelch (Kynaston Reeves). Campion was brilliant as Bunter, but was sadly typecast once he had established the role.

Michael Crawford and Melvyn Hayes all had parts in the plays and went on to bigger and better things but, sadly, Campion became somewhat typecast in the role he played so brilliantly.

Resident clown at the BBC for thirty years was Richard Hearne, who created the lovable Mr Pastry. Although he appeared on variety and revue, it was with children that he gained his staunchest fans. His humour was always clean, always well intentioned, and never in bad taste. Hearne was born in Norwich in 1908 into a theatrical family. His father was an acrobat and his mother a dramatic actress; he made his stage début in her arms at the age of six weeks. As a youth he appeared in circus and later went on tour developing his 'dumb' act, with its visual humour pleasing all nationalities.

Hearne appeared at Alexandra Palace on the Baird system in 1936, transmitted to just a few thousand homes. He performed such acts as 'Take Two Eggs' (a cookery demonstration), 'Shifting the Piano' and 'The Handy Man'. The character of Mr Pastry came from a stage show that he and Fred Emney were in called *Big Boy*, and was developed by Hearne as the bungling, optimistic clown. He was to star in many children's and adult's 'refined slapstick' sketches on stage, TV and film.

Richard Hearne's Mr Pastry was a classic comedy performance.

He copied one sketch from a comic called Tom D. Newall, with his widow's permission. This became the performance by which many remember him – it was called 'The Lancers'. In the sketch Mr Pastry was dragged and battered around the dance floor by imaginary dancers with whom he was completely out of step. He performed it on *The Ed Sullivan Show* on American television with enormous success, and repeat bookings followed for many years.

Puppeteers reigned supreme in the early fifties, not least because of Freda Lingstrom's great love of them. As well as those already mentioned, Sam Williams provided entertainment early after the war with *Little Grey Rabbit*, and in 1953 began *Saturday Special* with the parrot Porterhouse (voice, of course, Peter Hawkins) and Merlin, assisted by Peter Butterworth. The show was written by Shaun Sutton, then actor and stage manager, who a few years later was to be responsible for many classic drama productions and become head of the Drama Group on television. One other member of that 1953 show was a glove puppet who used to travel from Guiseley, Yorkshire, every week for the shows. Porterhouse's great rival in the show was the now famous Sooty.

Harry Corbett, a Bradford businessman with an engineering degree, developed the doll from one he had bought in Blackpool while on holiday.

93

Sooty and his long-suffering 'master', Harry Corbett. Miniature props became a feature of the programmes; Sooty had everything a bear could want, including a xylophone and an electronic organ on which to play his signature tune.

After his initial TV success on *Saturday Special* and *Whirligig*, Corbett was given his own show. From the outset Sooty never spoke, but contrived to get Corbett to amplify his whispers and produce such catch phrases as 'Izzy Wizzy, let's get busy – magic' used when performing one of his tricks.

His first shows were called *Magic and Mischief*, and the latter often predominated, but Corbett still managed to make the piece of golden fabric on his right hand immensely lovable. A new dimension was added to the shows with the introduction of Sweep the dog, who was able to take some of Sooty's wrath, which until then had been directed only at Corbett, usually by means of a hammer or water-pistol. Props became more sophisticated and more characters were added to the shows.

A particularly favourite memory of the programmes for many is the weary 'Bye-bye everyone, bye-bye' that Corbett uttered at the end of each show after yet another hammering or dousing. Sooty and Sweep glove puppets were ideal for commercialisation, and thousands were sold. Corbett was never short of a 'summer season' with his show for 'children of all ages'.

Families with televisions were still the lucky ones. For a couple of years I

Grown-ups had the Grove family on television and the Archers and Dales on radio. Here is the cast of the popular children's television family, the Appleyards.

ran half a mile each evening to my grandmother's house to watch my programmes on her twelve-inch Bush console. The walk home may have given me time to reflect on that evening's viewing and embedded such strong memories of those times. I was fond of Shirley Abicair and her zither and her homely tales of the Aborigine children Tumburumba and friends Tea Cup and Clothespeg. Shirley said it was quite common for Aboriginal parents to call their children after useful articles, in English, but it still seemed odd to me at the time.

The odd and unusual were featured in a short programme called *Stranger than Fiction*. The fifteen-minute films had a catchy staccato theme played by Bert Weedon, and always began: 'England is a beautiful country as well as a strange one. It has more oddities to the square mile than Alice's Wonderland, which, as you remember, grew curiouser and curiouser the more she looked at it.'

Peter Butterworth and his wife Janet Brown were often on the televison at that time. Janet seemed to be forever singing a song about a horse called Walter, while Peter, with his beaten-up bowler, wire-rimmed glasses, muffler and screwed-up face, was Mr Chadwicke-Bugle. He appeared to the

Whirlybirds was an imported adventure series shown by the BBC in the late fifties and early sixties. In America, where it originated, it only lasted until 1958.

sound of a bugle fanfare before he told his stories.

I laughed with Desmond Walter-Ellis when he was Mr Little at Large and at Saveen with Daisy May and his real dog Mickey, at whom he actually swore! ('Shut that ruddy dog up!') Then there was the excitement of Renfrew of the Mounties, who apart from being a number one shot was also an excellent cook and had a fine tenor voice.

The theme music of the serial *Stranger on the Shore*, which was taken to the top of the hit parade by Acker Bilk, brings back memories of the stories of a French *au pair* girl living with an English family – especially memories of their rascal of a son, called 'Podger'.

1953 saw a great upsurge in the interest in television. *Radio Times* was giving a whole page per day to the TV programmes, and it was in that year that the coronation of Queen Elizabeth II stimulated the sales of sets to such an extent that television could definitely claim to have arrived. Over 100,000 new sets were licensed, and magazines devoted to TV personalities and shows began to appear up on the bookstalls. In 1952/3 European television was born. The links developed in that year enabled an estimated 100 million viewers to watch the Coronation, which was given enormous coverage by the BBC and became the most spectacular (and longest) event televised up to that date. In the same year, the first Quatermass thriller was produced, *Panorama* began, and the first of the television 'families' was conceived.

The new family to arrive on children's television were the Appleyards. The show was initially written by David Edwards, and he starred in it with Constance Fraser and Douglas Muir. The successful format was copied by *The Grove Family*, an adult soap opera which followed a year later. The stories of the Appleyards were based on the exploits of the three children and their friends, which ranged from getting stuck in a lift to taking part in the London to Brighton veteran car run. Kevin Sheldon produced the programmes.

Two of the more popular series offered by the BBC in the late fifties and early sixties were *Whirlybirds* and *Circus Boy*. *Whirlybirds* starred Kenneth Tobey and Craig Hill as Chuck Martin and P. T. Moore. The wisecracking P.T. and the more solemn Chuck were two freelance helicopter pilots who became involved in chasing smugglers, gorillas, robbers, runaway children – you name it, they chased it. Photography from the helicopter was often spectacular, but the two stars never piloted the machine in reality. The manoeuvres and stunts were performed by pilot Bob Gilreath. In the early sixties *Circus Boy* proved a good training-ground not only for lions, tigers and pet elephant Bimbo, but also for young Mickey Dolenz (then known as Mickey Braddock) who played Corky, the circus boy of the title. He was later to become one of the Monkees pop group and eventually produced children's television programmes himself. Also in the cast were Robert Lowery as Big Jim Champion, circus boss, Guinn Martin as the burly canvasman Pete, and Noah Beery Junior – Corky's guardian, who later was to play Jim Rockford's father in *The Rockford Files*.

Peggy Miller scoured the world's television screens for suitable programmes to import for the BBC, and her finds from Europe included the adventures of a child detective, *Cristobal and Company*, films of *Heidi* and *The Limping Boy* and, for the very young, *Hector's House*, starring Hector the dog, Za Za the cat and Mr Kiki Frog. From Canada she imported the Tales of the Riverbank series, given British narration by Johnny Morris and featuring the exploits of Hammy, Roderick the rat, and Guinea Pig.

9

The Commercial Break

In the late 1940s and early 1950s the advocates of commercial television had many vociferous opponents, who looked at the sponsorship system in America and its often prosaic output and thought that any such system would reduce the quality of television here. Others, like Norman Collins, Controller of BBC Television, resigned their posts because they believed so strongly that a new channel would invigorate the new art and shake the BBC from its apathy about the medium.

The argument became a political issue, with Labour calling the prospect of commercial television a 'national disaster', while Conservative feeling was to support the competition that any new channel would bring. Churchill had not supported the findings of the 1951 Beveridge Report – which rejected the idea of commercial television in Britain – and in 1953, after coming to power, he initiated steps which led to the Television Act of 1954. By this Act the Independent Television Authority was inaugurated, under the chairmanship of Sir Kenneth Clark. The American sponsorship system was rejected in favour of straightforward buying of air time between programme advertisers. So what the Archbishop of Canterbury had tried to stop 'for the sake of our children' finally came into being.

It was on 22 September 1955 that ITV was first able to transmit to those viewers whose sets could receive the service. By that year it was estimated that 2,200,000 children were regular viewers, whereas only 1,500,000 still listened to Children's Hour on the radio; and this at a time when less than half the homes in Britain had a television set.

In a gesture almost of defiance BBC radio upstaged the opening of commercial television in the Press by the deliberately timed demise of Grace Archer in the long-running series *The Archers*. It was her death in the burning stable, trying to rescue her horse, that hit the headlines the next morning.

Associated Rediffusion and Associated Television opened in London, ATV covering the weekday programmes in London and the Midlands. On 3 May 1956 Granada Television opened in Manchester, with 'no names only a promise', and provided the daily service in the North. The weekend programmes in the North and Midlands were catered for by ABC, whose studios were opened by Janette Scott on 5 May.

The networks slowly established themselves, and competition with the BBC for audiences of all ages became keen. It was about that time that screen sizes of sets began to increase dramatically. Whereas in the late forties eight-inch screens were the norm, by the mid-fifties seventeen- and nineteen-inch sets started to arrive.

We were subjected to: 'You'll wonder where the yellow went when you brush your teeth with Pepsodent', 'A penny-farthing a mile and you travel in style – the Renault Dauphine', and the very first commercial break of them all: 'It's tingling fresh . . . it's fresh as ice . . . it's Gibbs' SR toothpaste'.

One of the first programmes for younger viewers provided on the new channel was Enid Blyton's already very popular *Adventures of Noddy*. It was in the field of entertainment for the twelve to sixteen age group that Michael Westmore thought ITV could improve upon the BBC's record. He had become Director of Children's Programmes with Associated Rediffusion.

The first programmes included a *Small Time* featuring Johnny and Flonny, with Paul Hansard, and another *Small Time* with Rolf Harris. Peter Hayes was the puppeteer responsible for the Noddy programmes and later for *Captain Kipper*, and Edward Andrews presented a similar puppet programme called *Colonel Crock*, which featured the adventures of old cars. There was *Buddy Budgerigar* with Peter Butterworth, *Tales from Hans Christian Andersen*, *Sport Spot*, Armand and Michaela Denis (two more fugitives from the BBC), Nat Temple (compèring as well as leading his band), a play by Peter Ling, and two cowboys, Roy Rogers and Hopalong Cassidy.

Another filmed adventure which was broadcast on the Sunday of that first week was to become probably the longest-running of all ITV children's series. *The Adventures of Robin Hood* was originally made to run for thirty-nine weeks. New techniques were used in production, especially in set design – developed by Peter Proud – which enabled a complete 26-minute programme to be made in four and a half days.

Many of the sets were made out of stock items such as serf's hut, elaborate staircase, and archways which were mounted on wheels to facilitate easy scene changes. It was claimed that a complete set could be changed in six minutes. The outdoor shots were filmed locally, the Walton-on-Thames studios being situated near historic Runnymede. Detailed planning in sets and props to produce as nearly perfect as possible replicas of medieval weapons, furniture and interiors gave what was a cheap production an air of authenticity.

The role of Robin was played throughout the series by Richard Greene. Greene, born in Plymouth, had starred in Hollywood films and returned to England to serve in the war and later appeared on the London stage. While

Noddy, already popular with children, became a television star in 1955.

Richard Greene's Robin Hood, handsome and heroic.

making *Robin Hood* he also appeared on American television in plays. For the Robin Hood series he learnt how to wield the long sword, crossbow and quarterstaff.

The female lead in the early episodes was Bernadette O'Farrell, who played the part of Maid Marian until this was taken over by Patricia Driscoll. Little John was played by Archie Duncan, Rufus Cruikshank and then by Duncan again. Duncan broke his leg on the set while stopping a bolting horse. Because he saved some children who were directly in the path of the runaway animal he received the Queen's Award for Bravery. Friar Tuck was played amply by Alexander Gauge, already a well-known British character actor of stage and films. He had even appeared in radio's *Mrs Dale's Diary* before taking over the heavyweight role of the loyal friar. Alan Wheatley played the scheming Sheriff of Nottingham. I still have my copy of the million-seller Robin Hood theme sung by Dick James:

> *Robin Hood, Robin Hood, riding through the glen;*
> *Robin Hood, Robin Hood, with his band of men.*
> *Feared by the bad, loved by the good,*
> *Robin Hood, Robin Hood, Robin Hood.*

The Robin Hood series was to be the first of many historical adventure films produced in Britain for the commercial television stations. Sapphire Films, the makers of *Robin Hood*, soon set to work on another epic about the exploits of Sir Lancelot. William Russell played the adventurous knight and Jane Hylton was Queen Guinevere. Bruce Seton, better known for his role as Fabian of the Yard, was King Arthur in the series. As with *Robin Hood*, all the weaponry was real, but the armour proved too heavy, and rubber replicas were made. Russell played Sir Lancelot as a cultured, almost suave hero, but all the female acquaintances of this most eligible male were treated on a purely platonic basis in deference to the younger viewers, who much preferred action to romance.

Next off the Sapphire Films drawing-board came marine adventure with *The Buccaneers*, stories of dark deeds on the high seas. Robert Shaw came to prominence as the reformed pirate Dan Tempest. Roger Moore was to get one of the first breaks of his career when he took the title role in *Ivanhoe*, the next adventure series to reach ITV. Robert Brown played Garth. The series was not as successful as *Robin Hood* continued to be, and Moore said after its end that 'no one seemed to know what we were doing, and we all stumbled about feeling like boy scouts dressed up in armour'.

Another historical drama was sustained by Robert Newton's flamboyant characterisation of the eighteenth-century rascal Long John Silver. Robert Louis Stevenson's immortal rogue was given more good humour and honour than the author originally intended, and the parrot-carrying villain seemed as much intent on righting wrongs as on deriving financial benefit from his deeds. Kit Taylor played cabin-boy Jim Hawkins. Newton had played Long John Silver in the 1949 Disney production of *Treasure Island*,

and his interpretation of the part has become the model for all affable pirates.

The accent was certainly on adventure in the late fifties. As well as the historical settings, there were thrills from the African bush with such series as *White Hunter*, starring Rhodes Reason, and *Jungle Boy*, which began its long run on ITV in January 1959. The Jungle Boy stories were on the conservation of wildlife theme, which was not surprising as they were written by naturalist Michael Carr Hartley, who owned a 30,000-acre reserve in Kenya. His son, fourteen-year-old Michael Jnr, starred as the Jungle Boy along with Robert Adam, who played Doc Lawrence or 'Doctor Father' as he was called by the pidgin-English-speaking youth. Other regulars on the programmes were Cheetah, a lion called Simba and various other wild animals kept as pets. The series was filmed entirely on location in Africa.

Next came the *Adventures of William Tell*, with Conrad Phillips as the Swiss hero fighting the oppressive Lamberger Gessler, played by Willoughby Goddard. Jennifer Jayne played Tell's wife and Nigel Green was the loyal Bear. In 1962 we were back on the oceans again with Sir Francis Drake, with a series of new swashbuckling stories of this famous English bowls player. Not content with merely defeating the Spanish Armada, Terence Morgan as Drake became involved with other less important events in British nautical history. Jean Kent played Queen Elizabeth I, often aloof and with perpetually pursed lips, but occasionally managing to exchange a wry, knowing smile with our hero.

New British adventure serials all but disappeared from the screen in the sixties, but commercial TV relied on old favourites. Both channels took advantage of the stream of adventure being churned out by American studios. Numerous Westerns continued to be imported and with them many other sagas of escapist heroism. *Superman* and *Flash Gordon*, originally produced for the cinema, were serialised on some ITV channels. ITV also presented *Jungle Jim* starring Johnny Weissmuller, the adventures of the Little Rascals starring Spanky Macfarland, and *Hawkeye and the Last of the Mohicans*, which starred John Hart and Lon Chaney Junior as Hawkeye's sometimes faithful Indian companion Chingachogook. Another series in a similar vein was *Tomahawk*, based on the diaries of Pierre Esprit Radisson.

Roger Moore before The Saint and James Bond. Here he is the dashing Ivanhoe.

10
At Home on the Range

A fiery horse with the speed of light,
a cloud of dust and the hearty Hi Ho Silver.
The Lone Ranger – with his faithful companion Tonto,
the daring and resourceful rider of the plains
led the rightful law and order in the early West.
Return with us now to those thrilling days of yesteryear.
The Lone Ranger rides again. (gunshot)

So started the famous Lone Ranger series presented on BBC children's television. The excited strains of the 'William Tell Overture' heralded the appearance of one of the many cowboy characters to grace our screens in the fifties and sixties.

As early as 1928 E. Le Breton Martin had written and read stories under the title *Scenes from the Far West* on 2LO. Charles Chilton's *Riders of the Range*, conceived as documentary drama, had become extremely popular on radio, and from the very first weeks of post-war television Kit Carson and Tex Ritter films appeared. I remember thinking it rather incongruous that in *Kit Carson and the Phantom Raiders* the villains, in Zorro-like costumes, came galloping out of their subterranean den singing: 'We are the phantom raiders . . .'

Often in the fifties 'real' cowboys like Cal McCord and Ross Salmon demonstrated rope tricks or told stories of the Wild West. It was the imported films from America, however, which made the 1950s the heyday of cowboy drama on British screens.

The Lone Ranger was the brainchild of Californian radio station owner George Trendle and writer Fran Striker. He was heard first on station WXYZ in January 1933 and, much to the surprise of his creators, became an overnight success. Over 3000 radio episodes followed! When the serials were televised Clayton Moore took the part of the Ranger, with Jay Silverheels as Tonto. Silverheels was a full-blooded Mohawk Indian, and stayed in buckskins for the whole of the five years that the serials were filmed. The plots were always simple; good always triumphed and someone

Clayton Moore as the Lone Ranger on Silver. The creator, Fran Striker,
tried 'Hi Yi, Yippy Silver, away', then 'Now cut loose and away' before he
settled on 'Hi Yo, Silver, away!'

always asked at the end of the show 'Who was that masked man?' – a line which has given rise to a multitude of parodies. The Lone Ranger, or as Tonto called him Kemo Sabay (or alternatively Quimo Sabey), rode his horse Silver through seventy-eight episodes, most of which were repeated on BBC children's programmes for over a decade. Hi Yo, Silver, away!

Roy Rogers and Hopalong Cassidy were the gunslinging rivals of the Lone Ranger on independent television. They had both appeared in the first week of broadcasting on the new channel in 1955. The first Rogers TV shows had been made in America in 1950/51 specifically for the children's television market. They were all action and in America were used to promote commercial spin-offs. Rogers was born Leonard Slye in Ohio in 1912 and began his career as a singer calling himself Dick Weston. He had become famous as Roy Rogers in feature films before the television programmes, as had his wife Dale Evans, his horse Trigger, and his German shepherd dog Bullet.

William Boyd had also made his name in films as the legendary Hopalong Cassidy long before TV began using edited versions of his feature films. He later went on to produce and market his own TV programmes. Cassidy was a more mature figure, and his half-hour shows were less violent than those of some of his contemporaries; he deliberately set out with a purpose in each film – to show the difference between good and evil.

While Rogers was always resplendent in rhinestones and glitter, Boyd always dressed in an all-black suit and sported two pearl-handled revolvers. Other actors in the Cassidy series were Russell Hayden as Lucky, Andy Clyde as California, Edgar Buchanan as Red Connors, and Gabby Hayes. Having mentioned Trigger and Silver we cannot neglect Hoppy's 'wonder horse' Topper. Just as the Lone Ranger rode off into the sunset at the end of each episode, so Hoppy went back to his ranch, the Bar 20, but Rogers signed off with a song, 'Happy Trails To You!'

In 1966 Cassidy films were repeated in a deliberate attempt to give a new generation of children the opportunity of seeing them. Planners said at the time, 'We feel the kids today are missing out not knowing this legendary TV figure who is much more than a simple cowboy. He's an international institution.'

The Cisco Kid had been played in feature films by Warner Baxter, Cesar Romero and Duncan Renaldo, and it was Renaldo who continued to play the role of the broad-humoured gunslinger in the television serials, always introduced as 'O'Henry's famous Robin Hood of the old West'. The part was played slightly tongue-in-cheek, the Kid being one who would joke and flirt with a woman a minute but who, at the first scent of injustice, would leap into action on his horse Diablo. His constant companion was Pancho played by Lee Cardillo, who provided much of the comedy and rode a steed with the appropriate name of Loco. Some idea of the popularity of the cowboy feature is shown by the 27 million Cisco Kid comics sold in the United States in 1956. As their signing off line the Kid would cry, 'Adios amigos!' to which Pancho would respond, 'See you soon, ha!'

Jock Mahoney as the Range Rider and Dick Jones as Dick West, the 'all-American boy', were a little more fond of a knuckle fight and a little less humorous than Cisco and Pancho, and actually the two performed a ten-minute stunt fight display on the rodeo circuit in America. The television shows were produced by cowboy actor Gene Autry.

Although the Gene Autry show was not shown as a regular series in Britain, a spin-off series did find a spot on British screens. This series was centred on Autry's horse Champion. The theme song, 'Champion, the Wonder Horse' became a hit for Frankie Laine in Britain. The shows concerned the adventures of Ricky North, played by Barry Curtis, and his Uncle Sandy, Jim Bannon, which somehow contrived to allow Champion or their dog Blaze to save them from a dreadful fate. Other shows with similar formats were *Fury* and *My Friend Flicka*. *Flicka* starred Johnny Washbrook as the young master, and the programme was introduced by a surprisingly beautiful theme tune. *Fury* starred twelve-year-old Bobby Diamond as Joey, and Peter Graves played Jim Newton, the ranch owner who had captured the black stallion Fury.

Just as successful shows were based on exploits of horses, so were they on canine adventures. Two of the all-time classic children's favourites were the shows featuring Lassie and Rin Tin Tin. While Lassie lived a rural existence, Rin Tin Tin had to put up with the more hostile environment of Fort Apache.

You may remember that Rin Tin Tin and his master Rusty had been discovered as the only survivors of the massacre at Fort Apache, and were looked after by Sergeant Majors (Joe Sawyer) and Lieutenant Rip Masters (James Brown). Lassie, on the other hand, was usually involved in more domestic adventures, with his young master Jeff Millar (played by Tommy Retig), his mother (Jan Clayton) and 'Gramps' (George Cleveland). Lassie, like Rin Tin Tin, had been successful in motion pictures, but after his début on ITV in December 1955 he attracted a huge following which contributed to the drop in the viewing figures for BBC children's programmes at that time.

Other Western series which followed the above early pioneers were *Annie Oakley* starring Gail Davis, *Steve Donovan Western Marshal* starring Douglas Kennedy, *Union Pacific*, *Boots and Saddles*, a series about the US Cavalry, *Laramie*, *Wagon Train*, *Wells Fargo*, *Tenderfoot*, *Have Gun Will Travel*, *Maverick*, *Gunsmoke*, *Wyatt Earp*, *Cheyenne*, *Rawhide* ('Head 'em up, move 'em out'), *Branded*, *Lawman* and many more. Apart from the first two on this list, the programmes were not usually screened in the customary teatime children's slot. One series that was, however, was *Bronco*, starring Ty Hardin. The series began on BBC children's TV in January 1960 after the Corporation had shown the fifty-minute episode at a children's preview at the Lime Grove studios. Comments from those previewers ranged from, 'He's so handsome – that's good enough for me' from a fourteen-year-old girl to 'a bit too goody-goody'. The general impression was favourable.

Bronco was a reasonable success in Britain for the Warner Brothers studios, which produced a large proportion of the Westerns on British television in the sixties, including the unique *Maverick*. It was unique in that Bret and Bart Maverick, played by James Garner and Jack Kelly, were the first two cowboys to be portrayed as cowardly, dishonest, poor shots and with low moral principles. For all their faults they remain a fond memory, especially in providing some of the funniest moments ever seen at a poker table.

Cowboy stories were just some of the programmes where violence reared its ugly head. It was a problem that had rarely arisen with radio, where the young listener is to some extent his or her own censor, imagining only what it is within individual experience and predisposition to accept. In television, the 'whole' is presented to be instantly absorbed by the child.

A survey of violence on the screen revealed that only 'slightly' less violent episodes occurred on children's programmes than on adult television, the difference being that in nine out of ten violent encounters children were spared the consequence of violence. Very little of the violence shown to children was between family and friends; usually it was between known, often stylised, adversaries.

Both the BBC and IBA have drawn up for producers codes of guidance concerning screen violence. One yardstick given in the IBA guide advises that children usually model their own conduct on those they admire and are naturally antagonistic to those they feel to be bad. This is doubtless true, and needs only a subtle development into 'children are likely to buy what those they admire recommend' to illustrate another of the dilemmas encountered by the commercial organisations.

The IBA code of advertising practice in theory aims to eliminate emotional blackmail. No product can be advertised which would be harmful to children physically, mentally or morally, and no method should be employed which plays upon a child's loyalty or natural credulity. Some may say that these last points are not being wholeheartedly adhered to when a well-loved star tells children which products to buy.

11
When Somebody Else Pulls the Strings...

The need to produce numerous economical entertainment shows for children, combined with children's universal fascination with dolls, models and puppets and the ease with which television could endow such puppets with the breath of life, made the use of puppets on TV inevitable. Puppets, like cartoon characters, can often be made to perform in ways that actors would find physically impossible, and in many cases this is their charm and attraction. Often the appearance, voice characterisation and mannerisms of the inanimate doll can produce more interest and amazement in the mind of a child than the efforts of the most experienced actor.

At the very start of television, puppets and cartoons were used in both children's and adult entertainment. Muffin the Mule, Alison Uttley's Little Grey Rabbit, the numerous glove puppets and marionettes in the *Watch With Mother* series, *Whirligig* and *Saturday Special* have already been mentioned. John Wright's Marionettes introduced Mr Bumble to the screen and, when the BBC moved from Alexandra Palace, the first transmissions to open the Lime Grove studios featured Prudence the Kitten.

In 1952 there was a series of stories about Winnie the Pooh using marionettes. Another popular puppet show of the 1950s was *Billy Bean and his Funny Machine*. The programmes consisted of the various functions of Billy's complicated machine, including such features as Yoohoo's cuckoo house and egg chute, a windmill, Talkometer, Phassabadassa Switch and Dorset-Faucet (invented by Mr Fawcett of Dorset). It also had a 'cartoonerator' which could 'magically' draw pictures. The 'cartoonerator' was, I believe, Reginald Jeffryes, who gave us Mr and Mrs Mumbo with Splat, the mischievous ink blot that came to life, and a penguin family that lived in Snowland. The programme also had a catchy theme:

Billy Bean built a machine　　　　*The motor sang chuggle-a-rang*
To see what it would do.　　　　*Chuggle-a-ruggle-a-rator*
He built it out of sticks and stones　　*Then suddenly a picture appeared*
And nuts and bolts and glue.　　　*On the funny old cartoonerator.*

Billy's voice came from Peter Hawkins, the puppeteer was Elizabeth Donaldson, and the show was written and produced by Vere Lorrimer.

It was only a matter of time before the BBC set up its own permanent puppet theatre under the control of Gordon Murray. From his 'tin shed' of a studio he produced the famous Rubovia plays, with such characters as Mr Weatherspoon, the King and Queen, and the Lord Chamberlain. In the centre of the studio was a stage raised four feet off the ground on which the puppets were filmed. Murray wrote, directed and produced the plays as well as personally filming many of the early series. Some of the plays presented by the theatre were very elaborate. Ruskin's *The King of the Golden River* was filmed in 1959 with ten sets, including a large mountain, and fifteen new puppets. Murray was able to eliminate strings on his cast by well-designed underfloor mechanisms. Later he used stop-frame animation in the Camberwick Green and Trumpton series.

Another animator whose distinctive films still enthral children today, as they did thirty years ago, is Lotte Reiniger. Her silhouette films were featured on both BBC and independent television. She began making them in 1920, and in 1926 produced *Prince Achmet*, the first full-length silhouette film. It took her three years to make and is regarded by many as a classic.

Production of her films involved hundreds of sketches and cut-outs, each wired so that the limbs and head could be easily moved. The cut-out figures were placed between glass and transparent paper and were photographed by Lotte's husband Carl Kock. A twelve-minute film produced this way required about 15,000 shots. As more films were produced so other artists provided background, but for fifty years Lotte Reiniger has performed the meticulous task of cutting out the principal characters.

Francis Coudrill, who created Hank, used a simpler technique of animated drawing by manipulating limbs, head and facial features on an otherwise static cartoon background. That method did not require the time-consuming stop-frame animation of Reiniger's work. Coudrill was spotted by Norman Evans and urged to on on the music hall stage. He had been a ventriloquist from the age of seven, and became a skilled painter as well as a science master at a Birmingham school. His work on the stage soon led to trial television programmes in the early 1950s. The 'Hank' spots usually began and finished with Coudrill ventriloquising with his Hank dummy but the adventures, filmed by Coudrill at his Beaconsfield home, were animated. Many of the scenes involved quite complicated mechanics with cams and cogwheels moving the eight-inch-high figures. Coudrill produced the shows from start to finish, including the music and all the voices.

William Timyn, better known to children as 'Tim', the creator of Bengo the boxer puppy, needed only forty to fifty drawings, some animated, to tell his tales of the mischievous Bengo. The stories were told by Sylvia Peters. Tim began the features in 1953, modelling the puppy on his own pet. For some time his ten-minute tales were part of the early *Blue Peter* programmes.

A similiar technique to Tim's was employed by John Ryan, who created the good-natured but somewhat simple-minded pirate Captain Pugwash. The adventures of Pugwash, with his motley crew aboard the *Black Pig* and his adversary Cut Throat Jake, began in 1957. The nasty situations in which Pugwash found himself were usually put right by Tom the cabin-boy, who sat smugly back at the end of each episode and 'said nothing'. The voice of Peter Hawkins, the excellent drawings and witty stories of John Ryan, and the jolly accordion sea-shanty signature tune have made Pugwash a favourite for over thirty years.

Oliver Postgate animated the drawings of Peter Firmin in the notable *Noggin the Nog* and subsequent serials. The wired-drawing principle was used to great effect, and the story and dialogue were particularly inventive. Postgate also produced the Little Watha series as part of *Blue Peter*, and *Alexander the Mouse* for commercial television. The Postgate–Firmin team were responsible for such well-loved characters as Ivor the Engine, Pingwings and The Clangers. Many of their puppet cartoon features were made at Peter Firmin's farm at Blean near Canterbury, where visitors could see, hanging on hooks, glove puppets of Ollie Beak, Fred Barker and Basil Brush – all their creations.

ITV relied heavily on puppetry and cartoons in their programmes for the very young. The *Small Time* series introduced a host of new characters for the very young, including Snoozy the sealion with Dorothy Smith, and Theodore, a rabbit who became a minor star, with his companion Larry Parker. Rolf Harris appeared on many of these programmes with his own brand of spontaneous cartoons.

In 1959 two series on ITV were to herald a newcomer who was to have probably the greatest success internationally with television puppets. The series, called *Twizzle* and *Torchy*, were both the work of Gerry Anderson. He had started in TV with Pentagon Films, producing advertisements with a young and enthusiastic team. When Roberta Leigh, a novelist then working for ITV, approached two members of the team, Anderson and Arthur Povis, with the possibility of making a children's series, they formed AP Films. The show, called *The Adventures of Twizzle*, was their first project. Reg Hill, John Read and Sylvia Thamm joined Povis and Anderson. When Read and Povis left the group the company was renamed Century 21 Productions, and still later became Gerry Anderson Productions. *Torchy*, the second series, was about a battery-operated boy who became involved in many science-fiction and more down-to-earth adventures. Characters in the programme included Mr Bumbledrop, a girl called Bossy Boots, Squish (an American space boy) and Pom Pom, a poodle who had to have her hair curled each night.

The next major step in Anderson's career was the series *Four Feather Falls*, which began transmissions in February 1960. AP Films had just enough money to make the pilot film and that was enough to sell the idea to the commercial stations. The programme blurb promised 'striking effects

Four characters in Four Feather Falls, *made by AP Films.*

and fresh techniques, making possible new strides forward in the art of puppetry'. The wires operating the marionettes were only 1/5000th of an inch thick and barely visible. The sets were probably the largest ever made for a puppet programme, with a 'prairie' stretching some thirty feet and a full main street, where the twenty-inch-high characters could act out their Western dramas. Lip movements were synchronised electrically for the first time, so that the voices of Nicholas Parsons as Tex Tucker, Kenneth Connor and Denise Bryer really appeared to come from the puppets' mouths. David Graham was another who provided voices for some of the numerous characters.

As is the wont of many human cowboys, Tex Tucker, sheriff of Four Feather Falls, sang the occasional song; his singing voice was provided by Michael Holliday. The puppet cast included a talking horse and dog, Rocky and Dusty, Pedro the Bandit, Chief Kalamakooya, Doc Haggerty and many more. Reg Hill provided the special effects, which included the shots from Tex's two magic guns. Michael Holliday recorded songs from the series, including 'Phantom Rider', 'Two Gun Tex', and the theme song:

> *In Four Feather Falls, Four Feather Falls,*
> *There's always magic in the air.*
> *But anything can happen, anything at all.*

The first of Anderson's space extravaganzas was *Supercar*. With Lew Grade's backing the programmes were to increase further the special effects and ingenious photographic techniques already developed. *Supercar* was first screened in September 1961 with Mike Mercury the test pilot, Dr Beaker a British boffin, Jimmy and his talking chimp Mitch as the chief characters. The total 'cast' comprised about fifty puppets, the largest assembled for any one series. Hugh and Martin Woodhouse wrote the scripts, the main theme being the help given to various folk in distress by Mike Mercury and his colleagues, aided by the remarkable invention the Supercar.

Next on the production line came *Fireball XL5*, with new stars Colonel Steve Zodiac (pilot), Venus (space doctor), and Matt Matic (navigator). By this time Anderson's team had become the leading authorities on their type of production, and had coined the term 'supermarionation' to describe the technique. In *Fireball XL5* views showing the puppets walking were avoided as this was difficult to achieve realistically, so they were shown travelling on hoverbikes or in their spacecraft.

Troy Tempest was the hero in the next series, *Stingray*, which took supermarionation underwater. Troy, with Marina and hydrophone operator 'Phones', headed the team calling themselves the World Aquanaut Security Patrol (WASP), waging a constant war against the undersea kingdom of Titan. Lew Grade's ITC had by now taken over AP Films and the thirty-nine episodes of *Stingray* were shot in especially rich colour, so as to look good on American screens where pastel shades were often

Thunderbird 2 *lifts off on another rescue mission. Even the theme music for this show became a hit.*

indistinguishable. In that series the production crew had to solve the problem of miniaturisation of water so as to make bow waves and splashes look realistic and in proportion to the models.

The problem was solved to some extent by adjusting film speed and by careful editing. Underwater sequences were filmed through a tank a few inches thick but eight feet wide and four feet high. The puppet action was performed behind the tank in which swam real fish and through which passed the requisite stream of air bubbles.

Arthur Purvis produced another puppet series for commercial television which was written by Roberta Leigh and came to the screen just before *Stingray* in 1963. It was called *Space Patrol*, and followed the tried and tested format of space conflict. In these shows Captain Larry Dart helped to maintain peace between the planets in the year AD 2100. *TV Times* carried a weekly story for children written by Roberta Leigh and centred on the adventures of Captain Dart and his crew.

Anderson's crowning achievement in puppet fantasy was to be seen in

A rare moment off duty from their Thunderbirds for all the formidable International Rescue team.

the highly popular *Thunderbirds*, with a whole new range of technical problems and exciting special effects. Jeff, Scott, Virgil, Alan, Gordon and John Tracy flew the mighty Thunderbirds, and the brilliant mind of 'Brains' the boffin made sure the machinery worked correctly. Another character in the cast was Lady Penelope, a female James Bond, who was chauffeur-driven in a pink Rolls-Royce with the number plate FAB 1. All were members of International Rescue.

In the first half-hour of the programmes the team usually found themselves in dire straits, a situation often contrived by their arch-enemy the Hood, but the second half-hour saw them safely back at base and revealed an explanation of the mysteries surrounding that particular adventure. The programmes were syndicated in the USA in 1966, and were readily accepted by American viewers.

That success was followed by *Captain Scarlet and the Mysterions* in 1967, and in 1968 by *Joe 90*, a brief departure from intra-terrestrial marionette battles. *Joe 90* concerned the amazing skills of a nine-year-old boy who

117

became a secret agent in his spare time. With another programme, *Secret Service*, the Andersons tried to combine live actors – namely Stanley Unwin (king of 'gobbledygook') – with puppets. Unwin, who played a spy priest, appeared both as himself and in puppet form. Anderson eventually turned solely to live actors and to outer space again in *Space 1999*.

The BBC has not yet provided quite such a sophisticated puppet show as those of the Andersons, but the *Dr Who* series has more than compensated the 'sci-fi' addicts. The BBC had more conventional puppet successes. Lenny the Lion ('Oh, don't embawass me!') with the help of Terry Hall, and Tich (joined later by Quackers) with Ray Alan were two ventriloquists' dummies to achieve stardom in their own shows in the sixties. Lenny was often helped by several guests in his show *Pops with Lenny*, while Tich was helped by 'Professor' Billy McComb and later by Tony Hart and Ted Taylor. His show developed into a quiz and was retitled *Tichpuzzle*.

In the mid-fifties Rolf Harris worked with Robert Harben, the magician and creator of the puppet 'Fuzz'. At that time, too, Michael Bentine created his Bumblies. They were from the planet Bumble and looked rather like large animated pears. There were only three of them, called One, Two and Three. One and Two were reasonably intelligent, but Three was a dim 'Eccles' character – the fall-guy of the trio.

> *Bumbley, Bumbley what do you say,*
> *Let's sing a Bumbley tune.*
> *Bumbley, Bumbley flying away*
> *And shooting over the moon.*
> *I'm Bumbley number one.*
> *I'm Bumbley two, that's me.*
> *I'm the one that's not very bright –*
> *I'm Bumbley number three.*

They all slept on the ceiling between shows, an unusual but none the less convenient pattern of behaviour. That was Bentine's first foray into the puppet world of television, but not his last.

In the late fifties two Czechoslovaks who had settled in Yorkshire in 1948 became famous as the creators of Pinky and Perky. They were Jan and Vlasda Dalibor, who were given a spot in the programme *It's Up to You* by Barney Colehan in 1956. The two pigs were hardly used in the act, and it was Colehan who suggested that they become a feature. With their animal friends they soon became known by their appearances in children's programmes and were eventually given their own show.

The basis of Pinky and Perky's performance was miming to popular records, but in their own shows with such 'straight men' as John Slater and Jimmy Thompson they were able to use their own recordings. These were in a similar style to those of the Chipmunks and David Seville. They also appeared at the London Palladium and in New York on *The Ed Sullivan Show*.

118

Florence, Dougal and Mr Rusty – owner of the Magic Roundabout – all awaiting the entrance ('Boing!') of Zebedee, who will surely tell them: 'It's time for bed'. BBC for the under-fives (theoretically).

The Telegoons, based on the *Goon Shows* of BBC radio, were another series of puppet films made in the 1960s. They used existing scripts written by Spike Milligan and Larry Stephens and adapted by Maurice Wiltshire. They were produced by Tony Young for Grosvenor Films. Although they were perhaps amusing to young viewers, the scripts were altered to give more visual emphasis and lost much of the originality and surrealistic wit of the radio shows.

Serge Danot created and animated *The Magic Roundabout*, and its cast of Mr Rusty, Florence, Dougal, Zebedee, Dylan and Brian were originally intended for a very young audience. It soon became equally popular with teenagers and adults, probably because of the droll, casual style of storyteller and writer Eric Thompson.

12
. . . and Draws the Pictures

As well as the flexible drawing style of home-produced cartoons, television was also supplied with cartoons from the Disney studios – *Felix the Cat* and other films originally intended for the cinema audience.

By 1950 Walt Disney had already formed the largest cartoon-producing company in the world, and had established Mickey Mouse, Donald Duck, Goofy, Pluto and numerous other characters, as well as his *Silly Symphonies*, in over four hundred cartoons shown in thousands of cinemas throughout the world. He had produced the first full-length feature cartoon with *Snow White and the Seven Dwarfs* in 1937, and followed that with such successes as *Pinocchio, Fantasia, The Reluctant Dragon, Dumbo, Bambi, Song of the South*, and *Cinderella*.

The BBC had transmitted extracts from these on radio and occasionally on television, but the Disney Studios refused transmission in Britain of any full-length cartoon, although cleverly whetting appetites with clips in preview programmes and specials. The shorts were distributed for television consumption and, as we have heard, Mickey was to close the TV service before the war and herald a new era after it. The cartoons were more often transmitted in the evening than during children's programmes. In the USA the studio promoted the Mickey Mouse Club, which has come to British screens only relatively recently.

ITV were the first to show the Disneyland programmes in the late fifties. These series of shows – sometimes cartoon, sometimes live-action adventure or nature – were among the ways in which Disney became involved in television, unlike many of the other companies, which were antagonistic to the new medium and initially refused to supply film footage.

In February 1956 ITV began to use some old Felix cartoons in a short series. The cat had been created by Otto Mesmer and developed by Pat Sullivan after Paramount had been interested enough in the original artwork to sign him up for the Paramount Screen Magazine. The first moving cartoon was made in 1919 and was called *Feline Follies*. In the second, called *Musical Mews*, Felix was officially named. With Sullivan's

'I yam what I yam, and that's all that I yam. I'm Popeye the Sailor Man!'

promotion, the cat's popularity grew even greater in Britain than in the USA. He was not, however, able to survive the transition to sound; in fact many of the visual gags were essentially due to the absence of a soundtrack – the antics of speech bubbles, the animation of punctuation marks. He had a few revivals, one in 1935 with a new series of cartoons being produced, and television showings in the 1960s. The comic strip continued for many years into the fifties but Felix eventually stopped walking.

Popeye was the first cartoon character to have his own television series in Britain. This began in February 1958. He had made his cartoon début in a Betty Boop film called *Popeye the Sailor* in 1933. Betty Boop was the creation of Max Fleischer's studio some three years earlier in one of their very first 'Talkartoons'. By the time Popeye was introduced, she had achieved cartoon stardom in films graced by the voices of Maurice Chevalier, Fanny Brice, Cab Calloway and others.

Popeye originally appeared in Elzie Crisler Segar's comic strip *Thimble Theatre* in 1929. After his first introduction with Betty Boop he was given his own cartoon, entitled *I Yam What I Yam*. May Questel, who had endowed Betty Boop with her squeaky voice, took the role of Olive Oyl, while the original voice of Popeye was supplied by William (Billy) Costello, with Jack Mercer taking over the character after the first year's cartoons. Gus Wickie was the voice of the early Bluto. When Mercer was unable to record some soundtracks, as he was abroad in the war, May Questel amazingly performed Popeye's voice for six cartoons.

The on-off love affair of Popeye and Olive, aggravated by the usually villainous Bluto, the innocuous hamburger-munching J. Wellington Wimpy ('I'd gladly pay you Tuesday'), and the amusingly irritating Swee' Pea, were the regular attractions of this long-running cartoon series. Their popularity was the result of their variety of plots, witty visual and vocal gags (especially Popeye's asides), clever use of music and popular songs, and the inevitable contrivance of our hero, by one means or another, to guzzle his spinach. The characterisation of the cast – especially Popeye with his eccentric mannerisms, gags and moral outlook – has possibly not been bettered in any subsequent cartoon series.

Some of his adventures, especially the two-reelers of *Popeye Meets Ali Baba and the Forty Thieves*, *Sinbad*, and *Popeye Meets Aladdin and his Wonderful Lamp*, are classics, having such memorable asides as 'Abul Hassan got 'em any more', 'Open sez-me' and 'Salame, salame, baloney'. It was the 'goons' who appeared in the cartoon *Goons of Goon Island* that inspired Spike Milligan to name his famous radio shows.

King Features produced 200 cartoons for television more recently, taking only two years to make them and, sadly, it shows. Much of the originality of script has been lost, although voices and some mannerisms remain. The original cartoons, however, remain as witty as ever, hardly dating in their humour.

Cartoons such as *Simon the Simple Sardine* had been made for BBC television, but the first cartoon on ITV made especially for the small screen was *The Huckleberry Hound Show* produced by Hanna and Barbera, which was first shown on British commercial television in July 1959. The programmes were shown at 6.30 pm, and because of that they were eagerly watched by both children and adults. William Hanna studied engineering at the University of Southern California and joined a firm building a theatre in Hollywood. There he decided to go to art school and later joined the

Harman–Ising cartoon company, where he met Joseph Barbera. Barbera had been a company accountant drawing cartoons for magazines in his spare time. Harman–Ising were producing cartoons for MGM, and Hanna and Barbera became a team developing the characters of Tom and Jerry and in the process earned their studio seven Oscars in nine years. In 1957 they got a telephone call in which they weretold that the studio was closing and that they were out of a job. They formed a company and in 1959 *Huckleberry Hound* emerged, using far cheaper production techniques known as 'limited animation'. This technique has been simplified even further over the years, resulting in mass production of an often inferior product by many studios.

The voice of Huck (who always wished us a 'Huckleberry Hooooooond dog howdy'), Yogi Bear (smarter than the average bear!), Dixie (one of the mouse duo, Pixie and Dixie), and Mr Jinks were all the work of Daws Butler. Daws had always wanted to be a cartoonist himself, but ended up on the sound stage because of his vocal talents – talents that had contributed to such Stan Freeberg hits as 'St George and the Dragonet'. He also provided the voice of Quick Draw McGraw, the next Hanna–Barbera character to appear. These shows had a similar format to the Huckleberry Hound shows with new characters including Daddy and Augie Doggie, Snooper and Blabber (cat and mouse detectives), as well as Quick Draw himself. These shows began on ITV in 1960.

Yogi Bear was also given his own show, and introduced the new characters of Snagglepuss (with his famous catch phrases 'exit stage left' and 'heavens to Murgatroyd') and Yakky Doodle Duck, as well as his old friend Booboo (who wasn't quite as smart as the average bear). In these shows they continued their raids on 'pic-a-nic' baskets in Jellystone National Park and their feuds with the park rangers. In 1964 Yogi appeared in a full-length feature cartoon in the cinema called *Hey There, It's Yogi Bear*.

Next to come from the Hanna–Barbera drawing-boards were the Flintstones, launched on British screens in August 1961, this time at 7 pm. Like the two previous series, these programmes, with dubbed laughter, were specifically made for the television market, but cinema audiences were given the dubious benefit of a production called *The Man Called Flintstone* in 1966.

The stories revolved around the domestic lives of two prehistoric families, the Flintstones (Fred and Wilma) and the Rubbles (Barney and Betty). Alan Reed supplied the voice of Fred ('Yabbadabbadoo') while Barney was Mel Blanc, better known for his Warner Brothers characterisations of Bugs Bunny, Daffy Duck, Sylvester and Tweety Pie. In 1961, Blanc was seriously injured in a car accident, breaking almost every bone in his body, and was unconscious for twenty-one days. When he regained consciousness he was able to read the many get well messages, including this letter: 'Dear Buggs Bunny, Plees get well. My mommy says you won't be able to talk any more if you don't. I love you. Lotty'. It was a year before Blanc could walk, and get back to his many cartoon voices. The same format as *The Flintstones* was taken into the future with *The Jetsons*, with equally predictable jokes.

The British team of Halas and Batchelor were to break the American monopoly of cartoons on ITV screens with their *Foo Foo* series. John Halas and Joy Batchelor created the shows for television, and the characters of Foofoo, Gogo and Mimi appeared in thirty-three cartoons in 1959 and 1960. The series, bought by ABC Television, were drawn in a very simple, stylised form and revolved around the eternal triangle of Foofoo, 'the cheerful but displaced citizen', Gogo, 'the rapacious villain', and Mimi, 'the overwhelming matron'.

The Bullwinkle Show started to be shown on some ITV stations at 10.45 pm in July 1962, and it was not until November that the time slot was changed to 6.10 pm. The hilarious shows became a minor cult, with Bullwinkle's regular 'pomes' being committed to memory. The programmes also starred Rocky the Flying Squirrel and featured Peabody's 'Improbable Histories', 'Aesop and Son' narrated by Charlie Ruggles, and 'Fractured Fairy Tales' told by Edward Everett Horton. The series was created by Jay Ward and Bill Scott. Bill Scott was a veteran animator from the UPA studios who, with others from that studio, made the cartoons for Jay Ward Productions.

The Warner Brothers studios provided television with dozens of excellent cartoons originally intended for the cinema, but did make a special series shown on British television – *The Bugs Bunny Show*. Individual cartoons were linked with introductions in a theatrical setting. Bugs presented the shows, often with disastrous consequences, rather in the fashion that Kermit later fronted the *Muppet Show*.

The programmes had a memorable theme written by Livingstone and David:

> *Overture, curtains, lights –*
> *This is it, tonight's the night.*
> *No more rehearsing and nursing a part,*
> *We know every part by heart . . .*

Other refugees from the cinema included Woody Woodpecker, created by the Walter Lantz studios; Deputy Dawg with Musky Muskrat and Vincent Van Gopher, created in 1960 by Larry Bourne for Terrytoons; Droopy, a Tex Avery character released by MGM; and Roadrunner, given life by the highly creative Chuck Jones for Warner Brothers Loony Tunes. Tom and Jerry, regarded by many as the most consistently inventive cartoon double act, were dependent on the pure visual humour drawn by Hanna and Barbera. Speedy Gonzales began as a cinema artist too, but could regularly be seen in the Warner Brothers TV spots.

Cartoon production for the cinema decreased in the sixties as TV, with its voracious appetite for material, took an increasing amount of studio time. The limited animation techniques of Hanna and Barbera were increasingly

124

copied by other animators as other methods proved too expensive. One cartoon character did develop in the cinema in this period however. That was the Pink Panther, who began life in the credits for the Peter Sellers film with that title and was so well remembered that his animators David De Patie and Friz Freleng decided to give him his own cartoon vehicle. He won an Oscar for *Pink Phink* in 1964, and a TV series followed.

In the mid-1960s the BBC found it had a minor controversy on its hands when it began showing the Johnny Quest cartoon adventures. Complaints came from adults who thought the cartoons were too frightening in parts for the age group for which they were intended, even though at a preview many children said they found them less frightening than the well-established *Dr Who* series. By minor cuts both adults and children were satisfied with the shows. It was pointed out by Doreen Stephens, then Head of Family Programmes at the BBC, that old favourites such as *Grimm's Fairy Tales* were often far more violent and potentially terrifying.

One of the biggest successes for the BBC in the sixties was *Boss Cat*. Imported from the USA, where the title was *Top Cat* (the name of a British cat food), the programmes began here in 1963. Stimulated by the racket of the alley-cats near his home, Bill Hanna began sketching the main characters the very next day, and T.C., Benny the Ball, Choo-Choo, Spook, Brain, Fancy-Fancy and Officer Dibble were born. Originally screened at adult viewing times, the cartoons were later reacquired by Edward Barnes for children's programming.

Scooby Doo, The Fantastic Four and *Dastardly and Muttley* are three more of the dozens of series produced by the prolific brushes of the Hanna–Barbera studios.

13
Kiddi-Kult

The rather forced Americanism 'kiddi-kult' was invented to describe that inoffensive entertainment which here we might class as family viewing. The Nuffield Report, following a survey of 4500 children aged ten to fourteen in London, Plymouth, Sunderland and Bristol in 1959, confirmed that children viewed heavily between the hours of six and nine in the evening. This had not really come as any shock to those in the media, since for many years earlier Children's Hour was known to have a large adult audience and the early evening radio programmes were often designed for a family audience.

In the halcyon days when radio reigned unchallenged, there seemed to be comedy and adventure series every evening of the week. As already recorded, Charles Chilton, veteran BBC writer and producer, compiled the Western adventure serial *Riders of the Range*. It was he also who thought up the idea of the epic *Journey into Space*. He was an enthusiastic amateur astronomer with a small observatory in his back garden, and took great pride in the technical accuracy of the series. Today I might not feel the same but for me, listening to those exciting episodes in the 1950s, the outstanding feature was the sound effects. To my parents, the peculiar noises I would make when passing through the 'air lock' of the hall into the spaceship proper of the lounge must have seemed a little bizarre. My imagination was completely captured by the daring enterprise of Jet Morgan.

The 'tales of the future' starred Andrew Faulds as Jet Morgan, commander of the spaceship, with his crew of Doc Matthews (Guy Kingsley Pointer), Stephen Mitchell, known to his colleagues as Mitch (Bruce Beeby), and Lemmy Barnet (David Kossoff). Lemmy was later played by Alfie Bass, and also in the cast was the young David Jacobs.

Another of the classic radio serials was *Dick Barton – Special Agent*. The programmes began in October 1946 and ran daily, Monday to Friday, at 6.45 pm until 1950. Noel Johnson played the title role in this first daily radio thriller. Because of the huge juvenile audience, Johnson had to renounce smoking, drinking and women – even his housekeeper had to go! The mood of the show was perfectly set by the opening music – 'The Devil's Gallop' by

Charles Williams. Initially there were Dick, Snowy White and Jean Hunter, but by Episode 17 they were joined by Jock Anderson, and Jean later disappeared, leaving the trio who were to captivate millions for several hundred episodes. Because of the typecasting that Johnson suffered as a result of the Barton shows he remained anonymous when he played the role of Dan Dare in Radio Luxembourg's interplanetary competitor to *Journey into Space*.

One radio hero with his feet fixed firmly on the ground was investigator Paul Temple. He was created by Francis Durbridge, and the programmes, produced in Birmingham by Martyn C. Webster from 1938, originally starred Hugh Morton in the title role. Steve was originally played by Bernadette Hodgson; after the war Barry Morse took the lead and Marjorie Westbury became Steve. Kim Peacock was Temple for the next series and later Peter Coke took the part. Whenever the strains of 'The Coronation Scot' sped through our speakers we knew we were in for half an hour of intrigue and suspense.

Another series in a similar vein was the adventures of one Archibald Berkeley Willoughby – alias PC 49. Brian Reece played the untypical British bobby and Joy Sheldon his fiancée Joan in the programmes, which began in October 1946.

Variety in the early days
In the 1920s, the only light entertainment shows were the concert parties such as *Elite*, *The Crotchets* and *The Valve Set Concert Party*, and their content was not that which would have consistently pleased a juvenile audience. The concept of a family audience was impracticable in the very early days, since each listener needed individual headphones to hear the broadcasts, but A. J. Alan's stories and the comedy of John Henry and Blossom, Tommy Handley, Charles Penrose, Jeanne de Casalis and Arthur Marshall must have amused children and adults alike.

Before 1938, there were very few regular variety shows, the best remembered being *Monday Night at Seven* and its sequels; but in that year Arthur Askey and Richard ('Stinker') Murdoch teamed up for *Bandwagon*. The show was the idea of John Watt and was produced by Gordon Crier and Harry S. Pepper. The pressure of the popularity of some European commercial radio stations had stimulated the BBC to present more regular lighthearted shows.

After a shaky start, the much talked about but never heard characters of Mrs Bagwash, her daughter Nausea, Lewis the goat, and pigeons Lucy and Basil became firm favourites. Syd Walker asked each week, 'What would you do, chum?' about some social problem on his mind, and Chestnut Corner enabled Askey and Murdoch to unload some corny gags on a devoted audience. The pair only had fifteen minutes of the hour-long show – but there was no doubt that it was their show, just as its famous successor was Tommy Handley's.

ITMA (*It's That Man Again*) was designed to catch the *Bandwagon* audience and duly replaced it as radio's most popular programme. The *ITMA* catchphrases and wartime popularity are legend, with probably more written about it than any other comedy show before or since. It is difficult for present-day listeners to grasp why *ITMA*'s ratings were so consistently high. But it undoubtedly helped to keep a nation's spirits high when they could have been at their lowest ebb.

Ted Kavanagh, writing the scripts, 'got away with murder', using literally dozens of catch phrases in each show and thus engendering a conditioned reflex both in the studio audience and at home. Someone once claimed to have counted seventy catch phrases in one show! To mention just a few: 'I don't mind if I do' – Colonel Chinstrap; 'Excuse, please' and 'I go; I come back' – Ali Cop; 'It's being so cheerful as keeps me happy' – Mona Lott; 'Boss, boss, sumpin' terrible's happened' – Sam Scram; '. . . but I'm all right now' – Sophie Tuckshop; 'Well I'll go to the foot of our stairs' – Tommy Handley; 'After you, Claude,' 'No, after you, Cecil' – Horace Percival and Jack Train; and the most famous one of all, 'Can I do you now, sir?' – Mrs Mopp.

Other wartime comedy shows included *Stand Easy*, Eric Barker's *HMS Waterlogged*, *Garrison Theatre*, *Much Binding in the Marsh*, *Mr Muddlecombe* – starring Robb Wilton – *Henry Hall's Guest Night*, and *Danger Men at Work*. Much more about these and other wartime shows can be found in the books recommended for further reading on page 152.

After the war, radio comedy blossomed into new hybrids, some with their roots in shows started in the war years, such as *Waterlogged Spa*; *ITMA* went to Tomtopia; the *Much Binding* crew continued with the same catch phrases: 'Not a word to Bessie' and 'Good morning, sir. Was there something?'

New shows emerged with new talent: *Take It From Here*, *In All Directions*, and *The Goon Show*. *Life with The Lyons* starred the husband-and-wife team Ben Lyon and Bebe Daniels, with Molly Weir beginning her Maggie character and daughter Barbara Lyon always managing to fit in the line 'I'll die, I'll just die'. *Ray's a Laugh* starred Ted Ray, with Kitty Bluett as his long-suffering wife. Over its many successful years the cast of this series included Fred Yule, Patricia Hayes, Peter Sellers, Leslie Perrins, Bob and Alf Pearson, Kenneth Connor and Laidman Browne. It too had its quota of catch phrases, perhaps the most famous being, 'Oh, it was agony, Ivy', and the weekly question to Bob Pearson, 'What's your name, little girl?' to which came the plaintive response, 'Jennifer'.

As for *The Goon Show* – today it is looked back on as beginning a new wave of humour and is regarded as a never-to-be-repeated classic. At the time it was just hilariously funny, with phrases and actions to be relived next day at school. 'You can't get the wood, you know', 'Needle, nardle, noo' or 'He's fallen in the water' became the standard reply to any remark by a colleague. The show's madness rubbed off on all of us, and it's still there.

128

There was the hilarious confusion of *A Life of Bliss*, written rather spasmodically by Godfrey Harrison. The first series starred David Tomlinson, but then George Cole took over the role of David Bliss and made it, to my mind, one of the all-time great comedy characters of radio. Another of those unforgettable personalities was the diminutive Jimmy Clitheroe, who set a record for the longest running radio comedy show with *The Clitheroe Kid*, produced in Manchester by James Casey. The programme maintained a consistently large audience from 1957 until Jimmy's death in 1970. Even *The Navy Lark*, written by Laurie Wyman and starring Jon Pertwee, the late Stephen Murray and Leslie Phillips, could not quite match its duration.

Educating Archie was another of those unsophisticated comedy shows which were commonplace in the fifties and sixties but a rarity today. It was very much geared to a young audience, and a very handy show to persuade children to go to bed, if they were allowed to listen to it under the comfort of their eiderdown.

A ventriloquist on radio seems almost as ridiculous as listening to acrobats, but Peter Brough – and Edgar Bergen before him, with Charlie McCarthy – unquestionably succeeded. Brough, the son of a music-hall ventriloquist, worked the halls for years with his 'vent' act, but his dummy had no name until Ted Kavanagh christened it 'Archie Andrews'.

Archie's first broadcast was on the *Music Hall* show, and this was followed by regular spots on *Navy Mixture* and *Henry Hall's Guest Night*. In 1947 Brough proposed a show for Archie to the BBC, but it was turned down. Two years later he tried again, and this time the BBC agreed.

Educating Archie was born in 1950, with Robert Moreton as Archie's first tutor. The several series were loosely based on the attempts by various people to instil a little knowledge into the cocky little chap's wooden skull, as described in the programme's theme:

> *We'll be Educating Archie*
> *Oh what a job for anyone.*
> *He's no good at spelling.*
> *He hasn't a clue.*
> *He tells us three sevens*
> *Still make twenty-two.*
> *It's a problem you can see*
> *To be Educating Archie.*

The scripts were written by Eric Sykes and Sid Colin. It was they who developed the characters of the odd-job man, played by Max Bygraves, Monica and Marlene, played by Beryl Reid, and the tutor – later played by Tony Hancock who rapidly won fame with his 'flippin' kids'. Bygraves' catch phrases 'That's a good idea, son' and 'I've arrived, and to prove it I'm 'ere' and Reid's 'Goodevenin' each' were on the lips of all young mimics.

Hattie Jacques handled the female comedy in the early shows, with Julie

Andrews, then only thirteen, as the show's regular songstress. Other artists whose careers were given a boost by the show were Harry Secombe, Ronald Shiner, Bernard Miles and the late Dick Emery, who was even then using his 'Lampwick' character. Bruce Forsyth and Sid James also appeared in the late fifties and early sixties.

The show was one of the first in Britain to have major commercial spin-offs. Besides the annuals and books, Cussons made Archie Andrews soap, replica dummies of Archie with his striped blazer and grey flannels were on sale at all good toyshops, he was featured in *Radio Fun* and Max Bygraves brought out the successful 'Dummy Song' with Archie.

Other series followed: *Archie's the Boy* with Benny Hill, and later on television another series of *Educating Archie* with Irene Handl and Dick Emery.

Hancock's Half Hour, scripted by the two gifted comedy writers Alan Simpson and Ray Galton, has provided some of the classic radio comedy sketches, popular with all ages. The haughty but vulnerable Hancock as the simple man with delusions of grandeur; his foil, the conniving Sid James, Hattie Jacques, and Kenneth Williams in 'a multitude of roles' provided a consistently high standard of entertainment.

Referring to child viewers, the IBA policy statement on family viewing begins: 'There is no single time in the evening at which the broadcasters can be certain that there are not substantial numbers in the audience.' Thus they acknowledge earlier findings, including the fact that pre-teenage children watch more programmes after six o'clock than the earlier ones designed for them.

Several programmes have appeared both on children's television and in the early evening, and American imports originally made for adult audiences have appeared in Britain at five o'clock, and vice versa. *The Flintstones, Just Dennis, Biggles, Huckleberry Hound* – all ostensibly children's programmes – were often screened at 6.30 or 7 pm.

The United States seemed able to churn out programmes for this slot, and both BBC and (more so) ITV gave over much of the early evening to such shows. Most of the 179 episodes of *I Love Lucy*, starring Lucille Ball, Desi Arnaz, William Frawley and Vivian Vance, found their way on to BBC screens in the late fifties and sixties. *Sea Hunt*, which made Lloyd Bridges a millionaire, *Lawman* and *Interpol Calling* provided some excitement. Robert Graves starred in *Whiplash* and Paul Birch in the stories of truck driver Cannonball.

There was *Father Knows Best*, starring Robert Young as the head of the Anderson family, *My Three Sons* with Fred McMurray as head of the Douglas household, and then in 1962 something rather different. It was a programme about a horse that talked, but only to his owner Wilbur Post. Alan Young played Wilbur Post and his horse was the 'famous' Mr Ed.

It was in 1963 that *The Beverley Hillbillies* first hit our screens. The signature tune played by Lester Flatt and Earl Scruggs introduced the

130

family, whose fortune was made when they discovered 'Texas Tea' bubbling from the ground. Millions tuned in to see the 'C-ment pool', granny cooking grits and jowls, beautiful Elly Mae (Donna Douglas), whether Milburn Drysdale would get his come-uppance, and all the whimsy of the hillbilly family. Buddy Ebsen played Jed Clampett, head of the family, Irene Ryan granny, Max Baer Jnr was Jethro (and sometimes Jethrine), and Nancy Kulp the lanky, easily embarrassed Jane Hathaway.

Merchandising of products derived from television programmes began with the earliest programes of *Muffin* and *Watch With Mother*. *Sooty* was a £25,000-a-year business by 1968. Some of the £20,000 spent on each episode of *Joe 90* was recouped by his presence on Sugar Smacks, dolls, books, guns, cars, games and gadgets. For the trade, 1965 was a Dalek Christmas with their spin-offs, but 1966 was definitely a Batman Christmas.

Batman, the 'Caped Crusader', was reintroduced in 1966 as a send-up of the old cliffhanger serials. The show was produced on two levels: for the young child it was an exciting adventure, and for the adult it was a 'camp' spoof of comic strip cartoons. Each week Batman and Robin tried to counter the dastardly crimes committed by one of their many arch enemies in order to save the peace of their native Gotham City. Their foes included the Penguin (Burgess Meredith), the Riddler (Frank Gorshin and John Astin), the Joker (Cesar Romero), and Catwoman (Julie Newman and Lee Meriwether).

In the first part of each episode, Batman – played by Adam West – and Robin – played by Burt Ward – usually ended up caught in some devilish trap engineered by one of their adversaries. But at the same 'bat time' on the same 'bat channel' the following day they miraculously escaped and triumphed over adversity. Lavishly produced, complete with Intergalactic Scanner, Interdigital Batsorber, Chemo-electric Secret Handwriting Detector, Bat-cave and the famous Bat-car, and with '*Pow!*', '*Bam!*' and '*Zowie!*' captions of the old comics, the series was a huge success for producer William Dozier.

Another childhood hero given yet another lease of life in the sixties and seventies was Tarzan. This time the loinclothed orphan of the jungle was played by Ron Ely. The series was one of the most expensive in television history, suffering numerous mishaps, from torrential rain wiping out a complete village set to Ely falling twenty feet swinging from tree to tree.

The series to create the biggest cult following of any TV programme was the highly addictive *Star Trek*. Enthusiasm for the series was due as much to the intricate, thought-provoking plots as to the excellent characterisations of the leading members of the cast. There was James T. Kirk played by William Shatner, a superhero of the highest morals, tough yet compassionate. There was Mr Spock played by Leonard Nimoy, with brilliant logical brain but devoid of human feelings. There developed a common hope among crew and viewers that one day Spock might achieve emotional thought.

131

Dr 'Bones' McCoy was played by De Forrest Kelly, Michelle Nichols played the luscious Lieutenant Uhura, James Doohan was Chief Engineer Montgomery (Scotty) Scott – forever losing his warp drive – and with Chekov and Sulu and the rest of the crew they boldly went high into the TV ratings. Phasers, Klingons, being 'beamed up' . . . all became the language of the school playground. Today, long after the Captain's last log has been put aside, thousands of Trekkies enthuse nostalgically over the programme which changed their lifestyle.

14
Broadcasting in Miniature

Having originally only one hour each day for children's programmes, planners packed an immense variety into those sixty minutes. The result was a multitude of different aspects of entertainment and education from magazines to monsters, from music to magic, which can only be summarised here.

The studio-based magazine programme, by virtue of its unpredictability and range of topics, has been able to please at least some of the children some of the time. *Whirligig* and *Jigsaw* were two early shows with a leaning to variety. Among the items that Fuzz introduced in *Jigsaw* was a comedy double act called 'Mick and Montmorency', which featured Charlie Drake and Jack Edwards. The two had performed a comedy tennis sketch on the Nuffield Show on TV and were spotted by Michael Westmore and invited to his office. At that meeting Mick and Montmorency were born and became regulars on the screen for two years.

Studio E, a midweek programme occupying the full hour, was introduced by Vera McKechnie. It featured George Cansdale and his animal guests, Ion Trant exploring the countryside, a section on model making, and a young artist called Tony Hart presenting a strip cartoon about a baby elephant called Packi. Ion Trant continued with countryside features long after *Studio E* folded, and Cansdale and Hart have become famous names in the annals of children's television.

The Monday magazine programme changed its name to *Focus*, but still retained some old friends, including Vera McKechnie as host. Commander Stephen King-Hall returned to children's broadcasting with his 'Here and There' item, Barry Bucknell 'did it' himself, Percy Thrower talked about plants, and Patrick Moore spoke in his own distinctive style about astronomy.

On 16 October 1958 a new programme was introduced 'for younger viewers' by Leila Williams and Christopher Trace. Its title was *Blue Peter*, and John Hunter Blair conceived and produced it. It first occupied a fifteen-minute slot purely for the toddlers with two or three items especially on trains and dolls. The show became established in its Friday five o'clock spot in the early sixties, being followed in the early sixties by *The Lone Ranger* or *Junior Sportsview* (introduced by Billy Wright).

When Blair fell ill, other producers failed to maintain the programme's high standards until Biddy Baxter, yet another producer of *Listen With Mother*, was appointed as programme editor; with Edward Barnes and Rosemary Gill she began slowly to transform the programme to interest both older and younger children. By 1963 – when Valerie Singleton had joined Christopher Trace – the format had completely changed. There were more competitions and more projects to interest children and involve them.

On the last programme before Christmas 1962, Val and Chris were presented by Head of Television, Owen Reed, with a box tied with ribbons. Inside they discovered an eight-week-old mongrel puppy. She was called Petra by popular vote, and became the most famous pet in Britain, except perhaps, for the Queen's corgis. She was to appear on every *Blue Peter* programme for fourteen years. Jason, a Siamese cat, soon followed and then Petra gave birth to a litter of eight puppies, one of which, called Patch, became another show regular.

John Noakes joined the team in 1966 and soon became their travelling

Blue Peter favourites John Noakes, Christopher Trace and Valerie Singleton – with Joey the parrot and Patch the dog – sorting some of the 150,000 entries for their Paint A Poster competition in 1967.

daredevil. Within his first year he had made a parachute drop, and in 1968 he jumped with the Red Devils free-fall team. He became Patch's closest companion, and when Patch died Shep was brought into the programme, eventually to become John's regular companion on excursions.

The cast's obvious attachment to the programme's pets was perhaps at its strongest between Petra and Peter Purves, who replaced Christopher Trace in 1967. Peter shook visibly when he had to announce Petra's death in September 1977. Thousands of children had written in pleading that Petra should not be 'put to sleep' when it was announced that she was to be retired. Every aspect of the dog's life had been documented, from washing, feeding, having her pups, and now her death. Children felt they had lost their own pet and the news hit newspaper headlines. Over her grave was planted a variety of rhododendron called 'Blue Peter'. A sculpture of Petra's head can now be seen in the grounds of the BBC Television Centre in London.

By 1966 *Blue Peter* was watched by 50 to 60 per cent of all children between five and fifteen years old. Just as with the Radio Circles some thirty years earlier, children's energy, eagerness and goodwill were put to very good use in the many appeals the programme launched.

The first appeals in 1962 and 1963 were for toys for children who otherwise would have had no Christmas presents. The target was to collect ten sacks and the response surpassed all expectations, with hundreds of sackfuls of toys distributed all over Britain. Seven and a half tons of silver paper were collected to provide two guide dogs for the blind in 1964, and an ongoing appeal continued for several years; four inshore lifeboats were provided for the RNLI by collecting 240,000 paperback books; over 700 million stamps were collected towards providing houses for homeless families. In all cases the children were invited to work or collect rather than just to send money, so that whatever their financial background they could all feel that they helped on equal terms.

The most amazing effort came in the seventies with the Cambodian Appeal and the first 'Great Blue Peter Bring and Buy Sale'. Here an exception was made when the presenters announced that the actual cash collected was a staggering £3,704,614 . . . The programme's organisers were able to send fifty-seven lorries, fuel, food, seed, fishing nets, vaccine, some 310,000 hoes, and numerous other items to the starving survivors of the Pol Pot régime.

In 1981 Edward Barnes, Head of Children's Programmes, pointed to *Blue Peter*'s twenty years of children's involvement as an example of all that is best in this field of broadcasting. He listed the awards won by the programme, which included the *Sun* Television Award five times, the Society of Film and Television Arts Craft Award (1969), the Television Critics Award (1972), several special awards, and in 1971 the Silver Heart of the Variety Club of Great Britain for the greatest children's programme.

The popularity of the programme was reflected in the Blue Peter Postbag,

Muriel Young, with Ollie Beak and Fred Barker.

a weekly section in *Radio Times* given over to listeners' comments. Lesley Judd was the next to join the team and, like those who followed her, was carefully chosen to fit the enthusiastic, outgoing image typical of the programme's presenters. The formula of quick-paced items of interest maintained its strong following, even when Thames Television began to compete in the late sixties with their new programme *Magpie*. This was initially hosted by Susan Stranks, Tony Bastable and Pete Brady, and was equally commendable for its wide range of subjects and profitable appeals.

Flickwiz and *Bubble and Squeak* were two magazine programmes launched at the very start of ITV. A year or two later, Neville Whiting introduced *Lucky Dip* – a children's newspaper. Musical correspondent was Bert Weedon, and Fanny and Johnny Cradock presented their 'Happy Cooking' section. Whiting was later to play Biggles in the series of the same name (co-starring John Leyton) and his place on the programme was taken by Howard Williams. The show was directed by Bimbi Harris. Williams, with Redvers Kyle, had presented an information programme some time earlier called *Enquiry Unlimited*. Muriel Young became another regular announcer on *Lucky Dip* and in 1961 was joined by a glove puppet, still at the time of writing on our TV screens, namely Ollie Beak.

In September 1961 *Lucky Dip* became *Tuesday Rendezvous*, with basically the same team. Fred Barker joined Ollie to increase the number of comic interruptions. The title of the show was changed again in 1963 to *Five O'Clock Club* (later *Ollie and Fred's Five O'Clock Club*), regularly broadcast on Tuesdays and Fridays. To join the club one had to be under twelve, and badges were issued to all members. Graham Dangerfield was the animal man, Jimmy Hanley made models, and Roger Webb and his group provided the music. Later Daisy the Cow joined the menagerie of puppet animals.

Stubby Kaye became a regular while on a sabbatical from America, and the show became modified for a time into a junior *Opportunity Knocks* under the title *Stubby's Silver Star Show*, a format used earlier in Carroll Levis' *Junior Discoveries* and several years later in *Little Big Time* compèred by Freddie Garrity. Marjorie Sigley, popular for her *Wonderworld* children's religious features, joined the programme in 1965 – it was then called *Five O'Clock Funfair* – and Alexis Korner provided the music. In December 1965 the name changed yet again, reverting to *Five O'Clock Club* with Muriel Young and Wally Whyton as presenters. The programme planners must have thought they had eventually got it right, for it then managed to survive several years without another title change.

The BBC pioneered television programmes for deaf children, beginning monthly twenty-minute broadcasts in 1953. The magazine programme obviously concentrated on the visual aspects of entertainment and interests, and necessary commentary was given in captions. Presenters were shown in close-up and spoke clearly, enabling viewers to lip-read. Children with good hearing were encouraged to watch with a sound commentary for them, but the shows necessarily tended to be taken at a slightly slower pace. The original title *For Deaf Children* was later changed to *Vision On*, and in these shows Tony Hart displayed his unique talent for improvised art.

Another artist who stimulated children to take up brush or crayon in the fifties and sixties was Adrian Hill. Through his *Sketch Club*, with his almost formal demonstrations, he must have inspired many youngsters to take a disciplined approach to art. Resplendent in smock and beret, with palette in hand, he was able to create, with a few brush-strokes or marks with charcoal, a running athlete, a playful dog or a country scene. So engrossed was he in his work that in the early days a gong would sound to remind him that the end of the programme was imminent! Several publications, competitions and a successful travelling exhibition enabled his audience to become closely involved with the programme – one which has never really been replaced.

Tom Tom on BBC provided a magazine for the older child, while commercial TV's *You'd Never Believe It, Enquiry Unlimited* and *How!* satisfied the thirst for knowledge of their older viewers. *You'd Never Believe It* investigated scientific principles, especially how they were utilised in the world of entertainment; a good idea, well presented by Arthur Garratt, resident boffin, and Huw Thomas, one-time news announcer, cast as the questioning and sometimes doubting Thomas. The show was a regular Sunday feature, and when Thomas left Tim Brinton took his place.

How! starred Bunty James, Jon Miller (gadgets), Fred Dinenage (usually providing some amusement), and Jack Hargreaves (authority on country matters). The questions were devised by Wendy Dickeson, who used her own family to test how interesting the items were. Questions ranged from 'How does an Indian tie his turban?' to 'How would you order a new aircraft?' Hargreaves later went on to present the Country Boy series, reminiscent of the Romany trips through the countryside.

The first 'pop' shows began in the mid-fifties when, as a result of a new-found freedom for teenagers and the universal appeal of rock-and-roll music, such shows were sure to attract a large juvenile audience. *6.5 Special* began in 1957, produced by Josephine Douglas and Jack Good. Jo Douglas and Pete Murray introduced the weekly shows, with Don Lang and Freddie Mills regularly in support. Tommy Steele, then with the Steelmen, increased his new-found fame by several appearances on the show, Adam Faith made his television début, and Laurie London had 'the whole world in his hands' after his first appearance. Skiffle and traditional jazz were heavily featured, but rock-and-roll seemed to be somewhat avoided, with the memories of ripped-up cinema seats still in the minds of the BBC's more adult viewers.

ITV soon countered with Jack Good's *Oh Boy!* and *Boy Meets Girl*. Regular stars such as Lord Rockingham's XI, Cherry Wainer and the Vernon Girls were joined by Cliff Richard, the late Billy Fury and Marty Wilde, who owed much of their early success to these fast-moving shows.

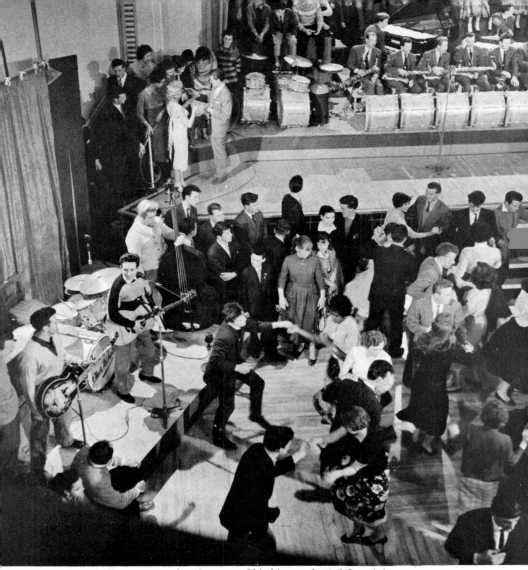

Lonnie Donegan performing one of his hits on the 6.5 Special.

There was more rock, reflecting Jack Good's emphasis on beat music.

Juke Box Jury on BBC enabled young and old to listen to the latest pop records, with David Jacobs asking a panel of celebrities (often more mature celebrities to attract an older audience) their opinions of the music, and to say whether the records would be 'hits' or 'misses'.

Janice Nicholls made her name on a similar assessment panel, this time on ITV's *Thank Your Lucky Stars*. Before one show she had just been a member of the audience, but her 'Oil geeve it foive' (a good mark!) expressed in her rich Birmingham accent became a national catch phrase. The show's compères included Pete Murray, Keith Fordyce and Brian Matthew.

Fordyce went on to compère *Ready, Steady, Go!* in 1963, but gave way eventually to the more trendy Cathy McGowan.

BBC's *Top of the Pops* has itself been consistently high in the ratings, even though it has stuck to its original and apparently dated formula. With both artists and audience getting younger, ITV launched *Discotheque*, presented by Billy J. Kramer, and later *Lift Off* with Ayshea, produced by Muriel Young for Granada.

Music and comedy were combined in the American-imported show called *The Monkees* about the zany adventures of a pop group of that name. The series was a supreme example of marketing and exploitation of the young masses. It set out to create pop idols and 'top twenties' hits for them, and it did just that in a blaze of international publicity. Davy Jones, Peter Tork, Mickey Dolenz and Mike Nesmith played the clean-cut goodies in a series of comedy adventures interspersed with pop songs recreating the style of the early Beatles films and music.

A glance through the pages of the television magazines of the last twenty-five years reveals an unbroken chain of animal programmes and items. The perennial interest in animals of each new generation has given rise to several long-standing series about wild and more domesticated creatures. The Bristol studios of the BBC have developed a speciality in nature programmes on both radio and television, and were responsible for the *Animal Magic* series featuring Johnny Morris. These began in 1962.

Granada Television first based an outside broadcast unit in London to present *Zoo Time* in 1956. The programmes were introduced by Desmond Morris, who had gained a degree at Birmingham University and studied animal behaviour at Oxford. The half-hour show had another star, however, in the shape of a chimp called Congo who became famous not only on the programme but also nationally and internationally as a painter. Even Picasso and Julian Huxley each bought one of his paintings! The programmes were later filmed and Chris Kelly took over the presentation.

Kelly was one of a chain of presenters to compère the junior version of one of television's most enduring quiz shows – *Criss-Cross Quiz*. In fact the junior version outlived its later-evening original. It was based on noughts and crosses, each contestant being able to designate a square on which to place their nought or cross if they answered a question correctly. These were asked by a long line of questionmasters including Jeremy Hawk, Chris Howland, Bill Grundy, Gordon Luck, Mark Kelly, Robert Holness, Mike Sarne, Peter Wheeler, Elaine Grand and Danny Blanchflower.

Blanchflower had introduced BBC's *Junior Sportsview* after his football-playing career was over, and later moved to ITV to host other sport-orientated programmes. Commercial television's longest-running sports feature was *Seeing Sport*, and was hosted on hundreds of occasions by Peter Lloyd. Every sport was shown in the half-hour in turn, each being described by a well-known sportsman in that field. Regulars on the programmes included Emlyn Jones and Johnny Leach. The programmes started in 1956

Desmond Morris, today better known for his books on human behaviour, originally became familiar to children as the presenter of Zoo Time. *He is seen here with the artistic chimp Congo.*

and soon were presenting their own trophy, hotly competed for by youngsters up and down the country. Bill Lato and Geoff Dyson were two of the regular coaching experts on the BBC's children's sports features.

We must all have our own memories of plays seen on television, whether it be the early *Man in Armour* or the Gordon Honour series starring Bruce Gordon in the fifties, the exciting Gary Halliday series starring Terence Longdon in the sixties, or the Orlando adventures featuring the late Sam Kydd. Perhaps you remember Colin Douglas as the simple, bumbling crook, Bonehead? Paul Whitsun-Jones was his frustrated boss, constantly having to change from plan one to plan two or even three and urging the unhurried Douglas to 'Act natural, Bonehead!' But it was on Sunday, when the BBC reverted to almost Reithian 'educational' standards, that the best drama was usually to be found. Sunday afternoon did not seem complete without the whole family taking tea while watching, for example, one of the Dickens classics adapted by Constance Cox, or *The Splendid Spur, The Secret Garden, Redgauntlet, The Three Musketeers, The Adventures of Tom Sawyer, Kidnapped, The Moonstone, The Black Tulip* or *A Tale of Two Cities*, the last of these being a children's serial giving Peter Wyngarde a fine chance to show his acting talent.

The excellence of some of these series was such that Clara Peggotty and her husband Daniel will to some always look like Edna Morris and George

In 1958 Elaine Grand presented Junior Criss-Cross Quiz *for Granada Television.*

Woodbridge, and a first vision of Uriah Heep played by the perfectly cast Maxwell Shaw is likewise an indelible memory.

The commercial stations, following the BBC's lead, presented filmed classics in the series *Tales from Dickens*. The episodes were introduced by Fredric March, and each contained an impressive cast of actors. Other Sunday presentations by ITV have been adaptations of *Black Arrow*, *Black Beauty* and – after an appeal by the then ITA in the late sixties for fresh drama rather than continuous repeats of filmed series such as *Robin Hood* – new notable series including *Tom Gratton's War*, *Follyfoot*, and the HTV 26-part serial *Arthur of the Britons*. In 1970 came the first unforgettable appearance of the eleventh-century Saxon sorcerer Catweazle, played by Geoffrey Bayldon.

Continuing the 'worthwhile' approach, the BBC presented *All Your Own*, a programme where children could show off their talents, whether singing, making models, building gadgets, or playing an instrument. Cliff Michelmore was the early producer, and Huw Wheldon introduced 'the children to the children' – to paraphrase Wilfred Pickles' famous line. Wheldon stood, forever questioning, fingers spread over cheek, the little finger bent to the corner of his mouth, nodding in obvious interest as small boys explained how they made a boat out of matchsticks, or a Japanese child demonstrated how to make tea.

A thirteen-year-old Japanese girl makes tea for Huw Wheldon: All Your Own, *1954.*

Eamonn Andrews, flanked by Michael Darbyshire and Ronnie Corbett:
Crackerjack, *1957.*

He was not averse to a catch phrase either, as with his concluding remark
he always described next week's programme as: 'Whatever else it will be, it
will be well and truly . . . all your own'. It was a programme on which I first
saw the random circular patterns produced by some child's
'harmonograph', and the first sight the British public had of the King
Brothers, destined to become famous pop stars in the sixties. A young
guitarist called John Williams also took his first step to stardom on the
programme.

Light entertainment has always been well provided for on both channels.
The first and longest-running show of this kind was *Crackerjack*. Freda
Lingstrom, Johnny Downes and Eamonn Andrews put their heads together
and came to the realisation that what children's television did not have at
that time was its own theatre, where a variety entertainment could provide a
pleasant time between school and homework.

The audience, from the outset mainly children, was encouraged to be
vocal, and had to respond with the word 'Crackerjack' whenever it was
mentioned on stage – for instance when the loser of any competition was

awarded the obligatory Crackerjack pencil. The response was almost Pavlovian!

The show included 'Double or Drop', a quiz where contestants were heaped with prizes which they had to carry throughout the questioning. Incorrect answers resulted in the award of a cabbage. For the first season there were Joe Baker and Jack Douglas, 'Mr Grumble', and Eddie Mendoza's Band. The show had guests, sketches, competitions and a final singsong where Andrews, always looking slightly embarrassed, opened his mouth but let the sound come from the other artists. Ronnie Corbett was another who joined the programme and gained valuable experience in television variety before going on to greater things.

Leslie Crowther became a regular and, with the late Peter Glaze, Pip Hinton and Jillian Comber, provided the entertainment with the Bert Hayes band for many years. Michael Aspel and Ed Stewart have also had long spells at compèring the shows. However, another show from the theatre, compèred by Jeremy Hawk and called *Hopscotch*, was remarkably shortlived.

On ITV there was *Little Big Time* with Freddie Garritty, *Nice Time* with Kenny Everett, *Junior Show Time* with Bobby Bennett, and in 1968 the trend-setting *Do Not Adjust Your Set (The Fairly Pointless Show)*. Produced by Humphrey Barclay, it starred Eric Idle, Terry Jones, Michael Palin, Denise Coffey and David Jason. The humour was as zany as one would expect from such a cast and featured the equally outlandish music of The Bonzo Dog Doo Dah Band, who were given a regular spot. It also featured the adventures of Captain Fantastic, which outlived the programme and were included in other shows.

Commanding interplanetary spacecraft, landing on distant planets, meeting and combating strange ghoulish creatures – these are the dreams of all modern small boys, and space travel, with its mystery and adventure, is today a reliable means of attracting a large audience.

In 1956 a young boy from Lanarkshire named Thomas Telfer had the idea of a television space club. Although only a teenager and with no experience of TV he went personally with his idea to Television House. There he met Peter Ling, then Head of Children's Scripts, who liked the idea and introduced the boy to Michael Westmore and Stephen Joseph. Not only was Telfer's idea used, but he was able to introduce the programme. Joseph became the producer and L. J. Carter was later brought in as technical adviser. The programme, which discussed all aspects of astronomy and space adventure, was set in competition to the occasional broadcasts of Patrick Moore on the same subjects.

Journeying away from science fact to science fiction, we find both channels fighting their own extra-terrestrial battles. ITV imported *Superman* and *Flash Gordon* in the 1950s, and later their home-produced serial *Pathfinders in Space* became very popular. The adventures starred Howard Williams, and because of their popularity a sequel entitled

Pathfinders to Mars was written. That starred Gerald Flood and George Coulouris.

The BBC filled this particular niche in children's entertainment with one major series. It began on 23 November 1963, and *Radio Times* wrote of it: 'Doctor Who? That is precisely the point. Nobody knows who he is, this mysterious exile from another world and distant future.' Even now, he is revealing new facets of his personality and powers, and after nearly twenty years we know him only a little better.

One of his lucky powers was his ability to transmute into another human form, thus enabling a succession of actors to depict the errant Time Lord. William Hartnell, who had not appeared on BBC television before, was the first Doctor in the episodes written by Australian author Anthony Coburn. William Russell played Ian Chesterton, a teacher, and Carole Ann Ford played Susan, his gifted pupil and the Doctor's niece.

The Doctor had been travelling in his timeship, the *Tardis*, when a fault occurred so he was unable to predict the time and location of his next landing. This continuing fault enabled the writers to present a wide range of different adventure settings, the most popular being those in the future – especially when the *Tardis'* crew were confronted by grotesque monsters.

The first Dr Who, William Hartnell (1963) and his assistant – played by Carole Ann Ford – confronted by Daleks.

Careful consideration was given to the presentation of the various monsters seen in the early programmes, for fear of frightening children. In fact just the opposite proved true; children took the monsters to their hearts, especially the Daleks, almost as fantasy teddies.

It was Terry Nation who, in writing the second series, introduced the Daleks. These gelatinous masses, enclosed in their pyramidal buggies equipped with lasers and other weaponry, became as famous as the Doctor himself, causing the streets of every city to echo with cries of 'Exterminate, exterminate' in rasping monotone.

The programmes were originally produced by Verity Lambert and always employed actors of noted ability, even to play monsters. Bernard Bresslaw played an Ice Warrior, and was acting alongside Windsor Davies, Peter Barkworth, Peter Sallis, and Marius Goring. Jack Kine and his special visual effects team dreamt up the shape of the Cybermen, the Yetis and many others; but always the return of the Daleks seemed the most exciting, and they even starred in a full-length feature film about the Doctor.

Patrick Troughton took over the part of the Doctor in the late sixties, with Frazer Hines and Deborah Watling becoming his constant companions. (Troughton was always known as Stephen Breck in our house, because of his stirring performance in the early BBC version of *Kidnapped*.)

When Jon Pertwee took on the role he brought some humour to it, and this trend was continued by Tom Baker, who played the part very much tongue-in-cheek. Then Peter Davidson portrayed a much younger Doctor. The catchy theme tune, written by Ron Grainer and concocted with the help of the BBC's Radiophonic Workshop, helps to maintain a continuity to the exciting happenings, which are still watched by the adults who nearly twenty years ago saw that 'phone box land in Britain for the first time.

Excitement, amusement, interest – such are the requirements to entertain a child. With television, perhaps more than with radio, the youngsters give themselves wholly to the medium. Television is largely a substitute activity – or so concludes an American investigation into the effects of the medium on children. It reassures, however, that there is no evidence that TV makes the child withdrawn, although it could reinforce those tendencies if they already exist. The one overriding advantage is the stimulation of young minds, which if correctly channelled can only be enormously beneficial.

It is somewhat reassuring that some of the most established children's programmes on both channels are still those simply telling stories. Stars of stage and screen, all excellent storytellers, have sat and read to the very young and to the not-so-young in series like *The Hot Chestnut Man* and *Once upon a Time* on ITV, and the long-running BBC programme *Jackanory*.

Jackanory has not only presented children with the best in short stories – beautifully illustrated by a variety of artists and told by actors and actresses with vast experience of the art – but has also encouraged children to read for themselves. Some seventy children's novels have been commissioned from works originating on the programme.

> *I'll tell you a story*
> *About Jackanory;*
> *And now my story's begun,*
> *I'll tell you another*
> *Of Jack and his brother –*
> *And now my story is done.*

15
Still Sitting Comfortably?

In this book I have remembered the developing years of children's broadcasting. Will today's personalities be looked back on with similar affection by tomorrow's adults? Edward Barnes, the man responsible for the 850 hours of children's broadcasting transmitted by the BBC, recently wrote: 'If you don't nourish and give space to the saplings, the blight will get them before they reach maturity.' He was expanding on the old adage about 'great oaks from acorns' in a way which shows that today's broadcasters are as well aware of their tremendous responsibility as were their predecessors.

Recently programmes directed at children have been given new slots in the week's progamming with the advent of Saturday morning television. This arrived with a bang on both channels as *Tiswas* and the *Multi-Coloured Swap Shop* competed for viewers. The BBC's *Swap Shop*, hosted by Noel Edmonds, provided a variety of slightly more sombre items than the unpredictable, custard pie-throwing action of ATV's *Tiswas*, which was most regularly hosted by Sally James. Both shows provided at home what many of the Minors Matinees did at the cinema for my generation, but with a lot more gimmicks and slickness.

Swap Shop, voted the top children's programme of 1977–8 by the *Sun*, featured a welcome throwback to the early days of television – a children's newsreel. John Craven's *News Swap* and weekly *Newsround* programmes began as an experiment in 1971 and, although they did not have a very encouraging start, by 1982 they commanded a regular audience of six million. Serious local and international news items are dealt with in depth, often with comprehensive background information.

The spontaneity of the very early Children's Hours has recently been rekindled in such shows as Southern TV's energetic quiz *Runaround*, compèred by cockney comic Mike Reid, the BBC's *Cheggers Plays Pop*, with Keith Chegwin, and ATV's wild *Tiswas*. *Tiswas* became as much a cult programme with adults as children, and adult programmes like *O.T.T.* grew from its juvenile humour.

Many programmes that started in the fifties and sixties still flourish. *Blue*

Peter, *Dr Who*, *Sooty* (now with Matthew Corbett), *Jackanory*, *Play School* and, with a slightly shorter history, *Clapperboard* and *Rainbow*. Some programmes on television may still remain; the last programmes for children on the radio are no longer with us. Lasting regard for *Listen With Mother* can be judged by the public's shock at the news that it was to end (in September 1982, after thirty-two years), to be replaced by a five-minute *Listening Corner*. A 2000-signature petition was handed in to 10 Downing Street, with Dorothy Smith, who read stories on the programme for twenty-six years, one of those who handed it in. The decision to terminate the programme was made by Monica Sims, as Controller of Radio 4, with Claire Chovil, Head of Schools Broadcsasting – two people with long experience of providing entertainment for children: Monica Sims as a former head of children's television and Claire Chovil on Children's Hour. It must have been a difficult decision to make, but they had to face the reality of a greatly reduced audience. (Nerys Hughes and Tony Aitken were the last presenters.)

A great array of programmes is now available for the very young on television. New characters like Bagpuss, the Wombles, Parsley, Hartley Hare in *Pipkins* (ATV), Bungle in Thames TV's *Rainbow*, and the occupants of *Hickory House* (Granada TV) entertain and educate. Johnny Ball's 'thinking' programmes, which began in 1978 with *Think of a Number*, fascinate a slightly older age group with the wonders of mathematics and of the world around us.

Modern video techniques have supplemented cartoons and puppets to bring fantasy to the screen in such programmes as *Jigsaw* and the comedy *Rentaghost* on BBC and *The Tomorrow People* on independent television. Drama for children has also provided more down-to-earth action in the serials *Maggie* and the extremely popular *Grange Hill*. The latter caused some controversy by showing children doing dishonest, cowardly and downright nasty things. Adverse criticism came mainly from adults, but the programmes were regularly watched by eleven million children – about seventy-five per cent of all those between the ages of five and fifteen. More conventional drama had included *Our John Willie*, *The Bagthorpe Saga*, *Carrie's War* and *The Phoenix and the Carpet* on BBC, and *The Jensen Code* (ATV), *The Flaxton Boys* (Yorkshire TV), and Enid Blyton's *Famous Five* (Southern TV).

Recent teatime trends have seen an early start to ITV children's television programmes, now called Children's ITV. To give it some coherent identity regular presenters have been introduced, Matthew Kelly being the first of these. BBC's children's programmes begin later, when there is known to be a larger juvenile audience (an additional three million are known to switch on at about five o'clock), and still attract twice as many young viewers as ITV. Certainly both channels spend vast amounts on these programmes, with BBC's average costs being £16,000 per hour – as much as similar adult programmes.

Audience involvement is a constant theme in children's programmes, and shows like *Jim'll Fix It* – with Jimmy Savile in the chair, of course – and Roy Castle's *Record Breakers Show* continue the tradition. But traditions may be on the verge of a radical change. With the advent of satellite and cable television and the increase in home video recorders, viewing patterns and thus programming are likely to alter drastically.

One senior children's producer has gone so far as to say that we may well have already lived through the heyday of children's broadcasting. If that is so, this retrospect may stand as a personal tribute to its creators.

Further Reading

BBC and All That, Roger Eckersley (Sampson Low, *c* 1946).

BBC Children's Hour Annuals (from *c* 1927).

The BBC Children's Hour Story, Wallace Grevatt (BBC, in preparation.)

BBC Yearbooks (now *Annual Report and Handbook*) (BBC, from 1928).

The Biggest Aspidistra in the World, Peter Black (BBC, 1972).

Broadcasting and the Community, J. Scupham (C. A. Watts, 1967).

Broadcasting from Within, C. A. Lewis (George Newnes, 1924).

Broadcasting in Britain, 1922–1972, Keith Geddes (HMSO, 1972).

The Cartoon, John Geipel (David & Charles, 1972).

Children and Television, Michael J. A. Howe (New University Education, 1977).

Children in Front of the Small Screen, Grant Noble (Constable, 1975).

A Do You Remember Book: Television, Burton Graham (Marshall Cavendish, 1974).

Educating Archie, Peter Brough (Stanley Paul, 1955).

The Effects of Television, ed J. D. Halloran (Panther, 1970).

Fantastic Television, Gary Gerani, with Paul H. Schulman (Harmony Books, 1977).

The Great Television Series, Jeff Rovin (A. S. Barnes, 1977).

The History of Broadcasting in the United Kingdom, Asa Briggs (Oxford University Press: Vol I, 1961; Vol II, 1965; Vol III, 1970).

Hullo Boys Annual: 1924. Contributions by Uncles Arthur, Jeff, Rex, Caractacus, Leslie *et al* (Cecil Palmer).

——: *1925*. Contributions by Uncles Toby, Edgar, Mungo *et al* (Cecil Palmer).

ITMA, 1939–1948, Francis Worsley (Vox Mundi, 1948).

Independent Television, Bernard Sendall (3 vols; Vol I: *Origin and Foundation*, 1946–62, Macmillan, 1982).

ITMA, 1939–1948, Francis Worsley (Vox Mundi, 1948).

Laughter in the Air, Barry Took (Robson Books, 1976).

Of Mice and Magic: A History of American Animated Cartoons, Leonard Maltin (McGraw-Hill, 1980).

Radio: The Great Years, Derek Parker (David & Charles, 1977).

Radio Times. 1923 on – notably Children's Hour, 26 February 1937; 50 Years, 28 September 1973; Children's Broadcasting Diamond Jubilee, 12 February 1983; Jubilee Supplement, 10 September 1983.

Schools Broadcasting in Britain, Richard Palmer (BBC, 1947).

Television and Radio (annual guide to independent television and local radio) (IBA).

Television Annuals, ed Kenneth Baily (Odhams Press, 1950–61).

Television – The First Forty Years, Anthony Davies (Severn House, 1976).

Those Vintage Years of Radio, John Snagge and Michael Barsley (Pitman, 1972).

Through the Years with Romany, Eunice Evens (University of London, 1946).

Walt Disney, Richard Schickel (Weidenfeld & Nicolson, 1968).

Who's Who in Broadcasting, Sydney A. Moseley (Pitman, 1933).

The Wireless Stars, George Nobbs (Wensum Books, 1972).

World Radio and Television Annual, 1947, ed Gail Pedrick (Sampson Low, 1947).

Index

B

B